Was Jesus Influ by Buddhism

A comparative study of the lives and thoughts of Gautama and Jesus

By

DWIGHT GODDARD

Published 2000
The Book Tree
Escondido, CA

Published by
The Book Tree
Post Office Box 724
Escondido, CA 92033

We provide fascinating and educational products to help awaken the public to new ideas and information that would not be available otherwise. We carry over 1100 Books, Booklets, Audio, Video, and other products on Alchemy, Alternative Medicine, Ancient America, Ancient Astronauts, Ancient Civilizations, Ancient Mysteries, Ancient Religion and Worship, Angels, Anthropology, Anti-Gravity, Archaeology, Area 51, Assyria, Astrology, Atlantis, Babylonia, Townsend Brown, Christianity, Cold Fusion, Colloidal Silver, Comparative Religions, Crop Circles, The Dead Sea Scrolls, Early History, Electromagnetics, Electro-Gravity, Egypt, Electromagnetic Smog, Michael Faraday, Fatima, The Fed, Fluoride, Free Energy, Freemasonry, Global Manipulation, The Gnostics, God, Gravity, The Great Pyramid, Gyroscopic Anti-Gravity, Healing Electromagnetics, Health Issues, Hinduism, HIV, Human Origins, Jehovah, Jesus, Jordan Maxwell, John Keely, Lemuria, Lost Cities, Lost Continents, Magick, Masonry, Mercury Poisoning, Metaphysics, Mythology, Occultism, Paganism, Pesticide Pollution, Personal Growth, The Philadelphia Experiement, Philosophy, Powerlines, Prophecy, Psychic Research, Pyramids, Rare Books, Religion, Religious Controversy, Roswell, Walter Russell, Scalar Waves, SDI, John Searle, Secret Societies, Sex Worship, Sitchin Studies, Smart Cards, Joseph Smith, Solar Power, Sovereignty, Space Travel, Spirituality, Stonehenge, Sumeria, Sun Myths, Symbolism, Tachyon Fields, Templars, Tesla, Theology, Time Travel, The Treasury, UFOs, Underground Bases, World Control, The World Grid, Zero Point Energy, and much more. Call **(800) 700-TREE** for our *FREE BOOK TREE CATALOG* or visit our website at www.thebooktree.com for more information.

FOREWARD

Christianity as we know it today differs from the eastern religions in many ways. There seems to be a huge gap between east and west when comparing religious traditions. Dwight Goddard manages to bridge that gap, however, with this revealing book.

Much of what we find in Christianity today had been added to the faith on top of the original teachings of Jesus. When we remove the additions and return to what Jesus originally taught, we suddenly find ourselves in a position to see things more clearly in relation to eastern wisdom.

What is interesting is that Buddhism has suffered with the same problems of additions and distortions over the centuries as Christianity did, and has also failed to uphold some of the original teachings of its founder. For example, the Buddha told his followers that he was a man, not a god, and not to pray to him after he died. Yet today, thousands of people pray to the Buddha for answers when he specifically told his followers not to, and told them they could never expect those prayers to be answered (at least by him). But the Buddha was a great man who still left behind great wisdom. A powerful religion sprung up based on his teachings and flourished half a millennium before Jesus was ever born. Five hundred years is a long time for a religion to spread and flourish, so Jesus could have easily been influenced by Buddhist teachings as proposed by this book.

Some would like to think that Jesus received all of his wisdom directly from God, which is one of the things that is supposed to make Christianity so special. But when Goddard examines these teachings of Jesus, strong parallels to Buddhism crop up in many cases. Is this just a coincidence? My advice is to read this book first and *then* decide. Goddard does a great job in revealing the parallel teachings.

Many years in the life of Jesus remain to this day unaccounted for. A few books have come out that strongly assert that Jesus had spent time in India, both as a teacher and as a student, complete with supporting evidence. Goddard also puts forth evidence that the Essenes, of whom Jesus had contact with and may have been a member himself, had strong Buddhist influences. If either (or both) of these scenarios is true, then the parallels between Jesus and the Buddha are more than just a coincidence.

Paul Tice

JESUS

This picture was painted by Bertha Valarius, who spent many years at the work before she called it finished. The painting is now the property of one of the Swedish Cathedrals.

CONTENTS

WAS JESUS INFLUENCED
BY BUDDHISM?

INTRODUCTION

FOR many years students, whose culture is not exclusively Mediterranean, have noticed very striking resemblances in the thought and beha-vior of Jesus to the teachings of Gautama, the Buddha.

To adequately consider the subject it is neces-sary to know something about the teachings of Gautama and the practices of early Buddhism; something about the life and teachings of Jesus uncolored by the influence of Paul and Second Century thought; and whether Jesus had had any possible contact with Buddhism or Buddhist influences. This latter question involves a study of the Jewish sect of the Essenes.

This book is written to present to the reader, in convenient form, material bearing on all these subjects. The work has been done in the hope that the reader will acquire from it a more sym-pathetic interest in primative Buddhism and a more intelligent discrimination between the con-flicting teachings of Jesus and of Paul and the Second Century John.

THE writer welcomes this opportunity of say-ing a word of appreciation and gratitude to those friends who have generously helped him in his studies that led up to this book.

To Dr. and Mrs. Edward S. Cobb of Kyoto, Japan, for generous hospitality, inspiring con-versations and valuable introductions. To Dr. Karl Ludvig Reichelt, founder of the Christian-Buddhist Monastery (Chin Feng Sang), Nan-king, China, for hospitality, instruction and in-valuable opportunities for making use of his ex-ceptional library, meeting the many Buddhist pilgrims that come to visit his unique institution, and for visiting with him many other Buddhist monasteries and thereby becoming acquainted with their abbots and sages. To Mr. C. C. Niah of Shanghai, for many courtesies, especially in-troductions to his fellow members of the Bud-dhist Layman's Association. To Secretary K. T. Chung of the National Christian Council of China, for very useful advice and encourage-ment. To Dr. M. Hina, late Dean of Doshisha University and now Lecturer on Christianity at the Buddhist University and the Imperial Uni-versity of Kyoto, for discriminating conversa-tions and introductions. To Dr. D. T. Suzuki of Kyoto, Professor at the Buddhist University and author of standard books about Mahayana Buddhism, for most illuminating instruction and the benediction that comes from meeting a wise, humble and sweet spirited man. And especially to Rev. Ekai Kawaguchi of Tokyo, a profound student of the ancient Chinese and Tibetan manuscripts, to whose wise instruction and council I am greatly indebted, and who suggested the writing of this book. I ask his permission to dedicate the book to him.

Dwight Goddard.

March first, 1927
Thetford, Vermont, U. S. A.

CHAPTER ONE

GAUTAMA'S BACKGROUND

INDIA of the Sixth Century B. C. was probably not much different from parts of India today. There were fewer people perhaps, but the contrasting poverty and riches, the farming, the crafts, were much the same. There were wealthy merchants, opulent princes, swaggering soldiers; there were men giving their time to the study and practice of philosophy and religion, some as teachers, some as priests for the ceremonials, and some as wandering and ascetic 'holy men.'

Caste was not so much emphasized as in later centuries but its outlines were everywhere visible. There were the Brahmin, the aristocratic descendants of the Aryan conquerors who even then prided themselves on their learning and culture. The Kshatryas were the military caste, they were also aristocratic and of foreign origin, either Aryan, or Scythian, or Mongolian. There were two plebian castes: the Vaicyas, or farmers and artizans and tradesmen; and the Cedras, or laborers and slaves. While these caste distinctions were not as rigid as in later centuries, the two aristocratic castes ruled over the lower in arbitrary and selfish pride.

The ruling religion of the Brahmin was the more idealistic part of Vedantism, which derived from the ancient poetry of the Rig-veda and the more recent philosophy of the earlier Upanishads. The religion of the great mass of the people was a mixture of Vedantism with the survival of still earlier crude animism and phallicism of ancient India. We may omit further reference to the crudeness of the popular faith except to point it out as an important part of the background of Gautama's thinking and teaching. It is necessary, however, to speak more at length of the purer faith of Vedantism. Buddhism from the beginning has been a Way of Life, an ethical method for escaping from or enduring the miseries of actual life; it was only secondarily a philosophy, and only incidentally a religion. The Rig-Vedas were an accumulation of religious poetry, not at all philosophic or systematic. As one writer said of them. 'They have a consistency of intuition rather than of logic.' Naturally the keener minds began to select the best of the Vedic thoughts and to idealize them. From the Tenth Century B. C. there began to appear philosophic essays (as different from religious poetry) that came to be called, the Upanishads. They continued to appear until the Third Century B. C. At first they were generally in prose but the later ones were all in poetry.

The close of their appearance was the Bhagavad-gita, the Song of the Blessed One. It derived from Upanishadic thought but was enough different to be generally classed by itself.

In their teachings they varied a great deal, even to appearing at times to be almost mutually antagonistic; their included thought was not at all systematic, but to all later centuries it has been a mine of rich ore; very divergent phases of later and modern Hindu thought have all traced their origin to the teachings of the Bhaga-vad-gita. In a true sense ' They represent the highest and purest speculative thought of India,' and it might be added, of the world.

But in spite of the rich variety of independent thought in the Upanishads, due to many writers in far scattered centuries, there can be discerned certain fundamental unities of thought. The old simple faith of the Vedic hymns is gone; to these deep clear thinkers a faith that only eventuates in priestcraft and the magic of cryptic knowledge, sacrificial ceremonialism to innumerable gods, and ascetic extravagances, is not sufficient. These writers were groping for some inner unity of thought that would bring light and peace.

How many gods are there, really, O Yajnavalkya? 'One,' he said. Now answer us a further question: Agni, Vaya, Aditya, Kala, Anna, Brahma, Rudra, Vishnu; thus do some meditate on him, some on another; say, which of these is best for us? And he said to them, ' These are but chief manifestations of the Highest, the immortal, the incorporial Brahman. . . . Brahman is indeed all this, and a man may meditate on, worship, or discard, also, those which are Its manifestations.'

The Self, Atman, the sinless, free from age, free from death, free from suffering, without hunger, without thirst, whose desiring is true, whose counsel is true, — that, one ought to investigate, that, one ought to seek to know.— (*Chandogya Upanishad.*)

The writers of the Upanishads as a whole are dominated by one paramount conception, that of the ideal oneness of the soul of man with the soul of the Universe. . . . the inner immortal self and the great cosmic Self are one and the same. . . . . What is real in each of us is his self or soul. What is real in the Universe is its Self or Soul, in virtue of which its All is One. . . . And the individual soul is one, potentially and ideally, with the Divine or Universal Soul. — (*Holmes' introduction to Radhakrishnan's, The Philosophy of the Upanishads.*)

While the thought of the earlier Upanishads is in the direction of monism, yet running parallel with it is a feeling after monotheism. An unknowable Universal Soul does not lend itself easily to worship, and as the philosophy of India has always been religious if anything, Brahma, very early began to rise to supremacy above the innumerable gods of popular religious belief and above the Cosmic Principle of the philosophers. In places this came out clearly: ' *I am the Brahman.*' ' *That art thou!* ' At the same time the human soul is sharply differentiated from the body and the rest of material nature. This assertion of the soul's enduring entity and its identification as an entity with the Brahman, the

Universal Soul, is an outstanding characteristic of Upanishadic thought of Gautama's day.

This thought carries with it the imperishability of the soul and hence its eternal life, but as death appears to end all, the early Vedic hope of some sort of eternal and heavenly life included the conception of transmigration, the passing of the soul from one body to another, and from one human body to some animal or some celestial body. The Upanishads united this idea of endless reincarnations with the ancient idea of retribution in a life after death for the deeds done in the body. The new idea of reincarnation in bodies on this earth, prepared the way for the distinctively Indian idea of ' Karma.' This doctrine teaches that the nature and conditions of each individual, are absolutely conditioned by his moral behavior in one and all of his previous existences. If he acts good, his rebirth will be in a good environment, if badly, in a bad environment. If he acts very badly, he may even be reincarnated in some animal body, or in some demoniac body in lowest hell. This not by the will of some god, but by an inherent law of cause and effect. While it is inescapable, it also forever leaves open the door of hope; a good life, all moral effort, will bring, just as inevitably, its just effect in rebirth under better conditions. Perfect justice is thus made a basic cosmic law.

One of the earliest Upanishads contains this passage: ' The spirit of man consists of desire. As is his desire, so is his resolve; as is the resolve, so is the deed (karman) that he does; as is the deed that he does, so is the fate which he attains unto.' Hence follows the supreme importance of the regulation of human desire.

This extreme emphasis in Hindu life and thought on the glorification of the soul, led inevitably to a dualism of soul and body, in which the body with its passions and desires was evil, a thing to be condemned and disciplined, and naturally resulted in a pessimistic view of life: all experience is evil and leads on to more evil. The soul untrammelled by body is alone capable of joy and peace. Hence a life of extreme asceticism, whose desire is ' desire of soul,' is alone worthy.

To attain this is the goal of life. It is seen as an attainment of unity with the One, the Atman, the Universal Soul. This does not mean extinction, non-existence, for the soul itself is atman and cannot cease to be; but the Upanishads plainly teach that the goal of realization is a state of bliss forever free from the tantalizing desires of physical existence. To this state was gradually given the name Nirvana. The word itself means ' extinction,' the extinction of the fires of desire. It was not until Gautama's time that Nirvana took on the meaning of extinction of form and individuality of soul.

From this early Upanishadic philosophy two outstanding cults gradually emerged from Vedantism: Sankhya and Yoga. In the former the emphasis was on the immortality of the individual soul as existing in a unified group, and hence of the virtual denial of the Universal Soul as One. This cult emphasized ' true knowledge ' through meditation as the best means of attaining to this blissful ecstacy of a soul forever free from body and matter. ' He who knows the supreme Brahman, unto Brahman he goes.'

The Yoga cult accepted the existence of the Universal Soul as One, but emphasized the practice of asceticism as the best method of attaining the desired end, namely the release from matter and the blessedness of union with Him. Many of these practices designed to accomplish inaction and lead to true knowledge were as old as India, but the Yogi so overemphasized the practice of asceticism as to make of it a magical end in itself.

It was not until after Gautama's time that a third method for attaining salvation, namely through faith in some personified form of Brahma, as in the Bhagavad-gita, or in Buddha, in later Buddhism, came into prominence.

In the Upanishads the ethical implications of its teachings were not worked out, ' they but revel in the fermentation of their thought.' It was left to the clearheaded Gautama, whose life and teachings we are now to consider, to elaborate them into a way of life.

From the Upanishads through the Sankhya cult he carried over a conception of a constant and orderly process of nature in which man, under a universal law of causation and the attainment of true Knowledge, overcame his handicap of ignorance and attained to release and blessedness; but he reacted away from the teaching of Sankhya concerning the reality and immortality of the individual soul.

From the Upanishads through the Yoga cult he carried over a conception of the supreme importance of the Universal Self as contrasted with the impermanence of the empirical self, seeing in the latter a significance only in its temporary reaction on the psychic process through Karma. From the Yoga, also, he carried over his ideas concerning the importance of ignorance, lust and clinging to self, as the causes of the miseries of life, and of the place of self-discipline in getting rid of them. He had very definite ideas as to the best ways and means for attaining quiet for meditation and securing trance and ecstacy, *but the importance of Buddhism does not rest on its Yoga practices.* While Gautama made such practices a vital part of his discipline, he did not advocate them to the extent of asceticism, he employed them temporarily and within reasonable limits, with enjoyment and anticipation of the end to be gained, which is, intuitive insight and blissful release.

The idea of Nirvana was taken over from Yoga, also, but Gautama gave it an entirely new significance that left it, in accordance with his characteristic agnostic silence, as to any possible life of the soul after death, and as to the nature of the gods, or Brahma, a mystery that might be interpreted as either ' nothingness,' the ' Void,' or as something ineffably rich and harmonious, the Bodhicitta, The Heart of Wisdom and Love.

In both Sankhya and Yoga these conceptions were held in intellectual aloofness and coldness, for to them all the misery of evil was illusion, and soul was not bound to matter. But to Gautama there was the most serious and intimate connection of cause and effect binding misery on the physical plane with the psychic process through Karma, and the spiritual process through love to an ultimate Nirvana. This is what gave to Buddhism its driving power and endurance and, while Gautama to the end of his life remained agnostic toward the deeper implications of the Upanishads, nevertheless they were in the back of his mind to enrich, by their presence, his thought and vision.

CHAPTER TWO

THE LIFE OF GAUTAMA

IF ONE wishes to make a careful study of the life of Siddhattha Gautama, he will be confronted by many volumes of legends telling of his miraculous conception and birth, divine attestations, miracles and absences from the body. Of one thing he will be very early convinced: that Gautama was a sensible man and a most lovable friend and companion. The books are filled with expressions of most ardent and sincere affection both for him and by him for his friends.

He was a very normal person in behavior. There was no exaggeration of self importance, no demand for deference, no fits of sudden anger or despondency; he was always wise, tactful and affectionate. The only things that hint at any ' psychic ill health ' are occasional trances and a comparative indifference to sex appeals; which can all be explained by the rules of the order in connection with self-discipline.

He was born in 563 B. C. and lived for eighty years to die in 483 B. C. His father was Prince of the Shakya tribe, whose little domain lay on the rich plains of the Nepalese foothills of the Himalayas. It adjoined the larger kingdom of the Kosalas to whose king the Shakyas owed allegiance. There is no certainty as to the exact racial origin of the Shakyas; it certainly was not Hindu nor Aryan, perhaps it was Scythian or Mongolian or Tai, no one knows. The Gautamas belonged to the Kahatriyas, and had slight affinity for the endless philosophising of the Brahmin, or for the superstitions of the Hindu peasantry.

His mother's name was Lady Maha-Maya; she was of princely ancestry, beautiful and talented. There are the usual stories of annunciation and immaculate conception; there were miraculous occurrences at his birth and the witness of the saints, all of which must be passed by as myths. It is recorded that she carried her son ten months and that he was born under a sal tree in the park where she had asked to be carried for the cool shade. She only lived a week after the birth, and the care of the baby was assumed by her sister Lady Maha-Japati, who was a secondary wife of the Prince, and who proved to be a wise and devoted step-mother.

As the child grew he proved to be of unusual promise, handsome, athletic and attractive, but sober minded to such a degree that his father became alarmed lest he should turn from the life of a military prince, heir to the throne of the Shakyas, to become the very opposite, a wandering ascetic, given up to study and meditation and self-discipline. The father did all he could to turn the boy's mind to the usual life of a Shakya prince. He protected him from all contact from the outside world, surrounded him by athletic companions, urged him to exercise and games, and restricted his studies under Brahmin tutors, and as he grew to manhood filled his evenings with the gaiety and pleasure of music and dance with fascinating girls. He was married at sixteen to his beautiful cousin Yasodhara, whom he loved after his restrained manner.

Gradually as he grew older, in spite of his father's watchfulness, he learned about the disagreeable things of life — sickness, old age, death — and he thought a great deal about their significance. One day he saw a mendicant, who was serene, dignified and without self-consciousness. The prince asked his attendant, the faithful Channa, ' Who is this man that is dressed in rags and yet who appears to be so calm and dignified? ' The servant replied, ' He is a wandering friar; he leads a life of austerity and begs his daily bread, but is without envy or passion.'

From that time Siddhattha determined to live a similar life of religious austerity. ' I believe that it will yield the fruit of a wise life and immortality,' he said.

When the father heard of it, he redoubled his efforts to distract the attention of his son. He added more guards and instructed the ladies of the palace to exercise all their charms, but to no effect. Siddhattha moved among the dancing girls and luxuries as unperturbed as though they were absent. But in his studies and in his athletic games he took a sober interest and excelled. He finally went to his father and talked over with him his desire to become a religious mendicant. His father said everything that he could to dissuade him, even offering to give him the throne immediately if he would give up his purpose, but in vain. He asked his father, ' Can you give me perpetual youth, or avoidance of sickness, or old age? Can you help me to avoid rebirth? '

One morning as he was being dressed word came that his wife had given birth to a son, and this after ten years of married happiness. He did not rejoice but is said to have exclaimed, ' Alas, another bond has come to hinder me.' So the boy was called, Rahula, which means ' hindrance.'

The same day when out riding he passed the house of a beautiful cousin who congratulated him and expressed her admiration for his attractive person; appreciating the temptation in it, he tactfully turned the conversation and later sent her a present, but the incident served to make still more clear the moral danger in his present life. That evening his father arranged a festival in honor of the birth of a son and heir to the throne, and the singing and dancing girls exerted themselves to the utmost to please Siddhattha, but he tired of it and fell asleep. Not being dismissed, the girls at last fell asleep themselves. When he awoke and saw their huddled forms all about him, clothing in disarray, hair dishevelled, and some with mouths open and snoring, he turned away in disgust and softly made his way out. He found his attendant and told him to quietly saddle horses and go with him. Then he went to his wife's room. intending to bid her good bye and to see his son. When he saw her with the babe on her bosom and both asleep, he feared to waken her lest his heart fail him. Then he went to the court yard, and with Channa mounted the horses and rode out of the gate.

They rode a long distance. Once he was tempted to return and give up his renunciation, but the depression passed and they rode on until they were over the river and the boundary of the kingdom, and they dismounted on the farther side. He removed all his jewelry and even his surplus clothing, gave them to the faithful Channa and instructed him to return to the palace and tell his father. Then he added, ' Do you comfort the king.' Channa protested at leaving him and sought permission to go with him. Siddhattha said kindly, ' If your love for me is so great, later on you may come.' Many years after there is record of Channa as one of his disciples.

Siddhattha evidently wandered about for a few months, alone and friendless, begging his bread from door to door. He lived for a time with Uddaka, a noted Yoga ascetic, but was bewildered by his severe and unreasonable mood of life. In answer to his enquiry the ascetic said, ' By pain they at last come to happiness, for pain is the root of merit.' This brought no satisfaction to Gautama for he was sensible enough to see that it led nowhere. They endured pain for the sake of happiness in a life which was still subject to death and rebirth. ' There ought to be some way,' Gautama said, ' of attaining to a state where nothing needs to be done over again.'

King Bimbesara of Magdaha heard of his presence and sent messengers inviting him to share his hospitality, but Gautama courteously declined the invitation and went to live with one Alara Kilama, a renowned Sankhya sage, from whom he learned the different stages of meditation and ecstasy. Alara taught a doctrine of Atman, the soul as identical with the supreme Brahman, which by meditation attained liberation from the body. This did not satisfy Gautama; perhaps he did not grasp the full import of the teaching. To him the idea of a separation of soul from body meant the survival of soul and hence rebirth. To him it seemed that everything, even the idea of soul, must be abandoned. So he left Alara Kilama and went to live on the banks of the Nairanjana river near the village of Uruvela. There he was joined by five ascetics whose leader was Kondanna, a Brahman soothsayer, whom he had met previously when he was a prince. These friends lived together for six years, practising an increasingly severe mode of ascetic life, until Gautama's body wasted away and he came near to death.

When he recovered he became convinced that there was no wisdom in such an extreme form of asceticism. He had become convinced before he started out that there was no hope in a life of self indulgence, so he concluded that the wise way of life must lie in a middle course of self-restraint and meditation. But still the problem of the soul remained unsolved. Was it an enduring entity as some of the Brahmin and Upanishads said? Or was it a part of the body to die with it? What effect then had Karma? and how could the merit of a good life be conserved? All these questions and many others pressed in on his mind. He determined to change the course of his life to a more moderate restraint and then to try and think it out. When his companions saw his change of life they left him in contempt.

Still weak from his years of fasting, Gautama rested under a fig tree. Sujata, the daughter of the village headman, had been in the habit of worshipping the spirit of that particular tree, and when she saw Gautama under it she imagined that he was the incarnation of the tree spirit, so she cooked some soft milk-rice and brought it to him. He accepted it gratefully but partook of it sparingly. For many days she brought him the food and he remained under the tree, thinking, thinking, thinking. One evening he determined to spend the night in meditation. '*I will not leave this spot,*' he vowed, '*until I obtain enlightenment.*'

Before the sun set he had a first encouragement, and before the morning sun arose he had the whole solution clearly in mind. The Great Enlightenment had come. The legends say that the first light came with the recollection of previous incarnations which had prepared the way for his present state. The second light came with a miraculous gift of 'the Heavenly Eye of Omniscient Vision,' the purport of which was that he had had a vision of the ineffable purity and wisdom and compassion of the goal of an age-long process. The third light came with a sudden appreciation of the universality of the law of causation; that it operated with perfect uniformity everywhere and from the first step to the last; that it was just as effective in conserving and utilizing good merit for upward progress as bad deeds for delaying and holding it back; but sooner or later Karma would *burn itself out* and there would be no more rebirths in this world of pain and suffering.

But this ending of rebirth was in no sense annihilation, for while the conscious mortal soul was impermanent and, in that sense, ' illusion,' and came to an end with the death of the body, yet through Karma it was tied in with the Universal Selfhood and, in that sense, was eternal. Not, ' as a drop of dew falling in the ocean,' but as an idea living and growing according to its own laws to gradually unfold into identity with the Universal Selfhood.

Thus was the idea of the oneness of the mortal soul and the Divine Atman, which Gautama had inherited from the Upanishads, made rational and consistent with his personal experience of pain and suffering in the world and the impermanence of the material body. This was the supreme enlightenment that came to him under the Bo tree, and which he was quick to see was available for all animate life.

From now on Gautama was known as 'the
Enlightened One,' or the Blessed One. He always referred to himself as 'the Tathagata,'
which means, the one-who-has-thus-attained. It
was not until after his death that he came to be
referred to, at least with its modern meaning of
divinity, as the Buddha.

GAUTAMA
ABANINDRO NATH TAGORE
Copied from *Buddha and the Gospel of Buddhism,* by Ananda Coomaraswamy
Published by George G. Harrap & Co., London, 1916.

BUDDHA

This type is symbolic of the serene, blissful, impersonal Buddhahood
—it is the goal of Nirvana, the Heart of Truth, the Womb of all Love
and Life. The seated figure is a modern copy in bronze, 11¼ inches high.
The base and nimbus are of beautifully carved wood covered with black
and gold lacquer of the Early Tokugawa period (Japan); it is 30 inches
over all. It is in the Author's collection.

CHAPTER THREE

LIFE OF GAUTAMA, (Continued)

FOLLOWING his enlightenment and still weak from emaciation and sickness, Gautama lingered near the spot where he had found the light, in alternate states of meditation and depression. The legends say that for forty-nine days the demons did everything they could to break down his spirit. After two weeks his strength began to return, and he could walk as far as the ' tree of steadfast gazing,' thinking, thinking, thinking. Then there was a week of almost trance in which he reviewed step by step his former re-births under the law of Karma. Then there was a week of great exaltation of spirit as he recollected and contemplated what he had seen in his beatific vision and ecstasy, of the ineffable sweetness of Nirvana. Then there was a week of reaction and depression, and a final week of re-assurance and readjustment, as his normal strength returned and the Golden Path cleared itself in his mind.

Close on the recovery of strength, as he was seated by the roadside, two merchants went by and courteously offered him food which he accepted. In the conversation that followed, he explained his newly found way of life and they were convinced of its reasonableness and decided to follow it. This encouraged Gautama and he set out to find his old teachers. Uddaka, whose instructions concerning Yoga practices he had found disappointing and unconvincing, he learned, was dead. Alara Kilama who had taught him the art of meditation, was dead also. Then he sought out the five friends with whom he had lived so long in ascetic rigor; they at first tried to ignore him, but later received him and politely listened to his words, with the result that their leader, Kondanna, was convinced of the truth and became the earliest of his educated disciples. This first sermon is still preserved in almost its original form, and as it was the model of hundreds of others it is advisable to study it carefully. It is called, if literally translated, *'Setting in motion the Wheel of the Law,'* but as that does not carry much meaning to western ears, it is better translated, ' The Address at the foundation of the Kingdom.' It treats of the Four Noble Truths which lay at the basis of Gautama's whole system of thought.

There are two extremes that he who strives for deliverance (*i.e.*, release from the chain of rebirth) should avoid. One extreme, the craving for the satisfaction of the passions and other pleasures of the senses, is vulgar, base, degrading and worthless. The other extreme, exaggerated asceticism and self-mortification, is painful, vain and also worthless. Only the middle path which the Tathagata (Gautama's usual name for himself) has found, avoids these two wrong ways, and opens the eyes, bestows insight, and leads to wisdom, to deliverance, to enlightenment, to Nirvana.

It is this Golden Eightfold Path, namely: right views, right aspiration, right speech, right deeds, right livelihood, right endeavor, right mindfulness, right concentration.

Now this is the Noble Truth of Suffering: Birth is suffering, disease is suffering, death is suffering, sorrow, grief, lamentation, pain are suffering, union with unpleasant things is suffering, separation from beloved objects is suffering, unsatisfied desires is suffering; in short the whole five groups of clinging is suffering.

Now this is the Noble Truth of the Cause of Suffering, namely: Verily it is this thirst, this craving for existence, and enjoyment which leads to rebirths; seeking satisfaction now in this way, now in that. It is the craving for the satisfaction of the passions, the craving for existence in this life or hereafter, or the craving for annihilation.

Now this is the Noble Truth of the Cessation of Suffering, namely: Verily it is the complete destruction, conquering, annihilation of these cravings.

Now this is the Noble Truth of the path which leads to the cessation of suffering: Verily it is this Golden Eightfold Path, namely: right views, right aspiration, right speech, right deeds, right livelihood, right endeavor, right mindfulness, right concentration. — (*Translation by Straus.*)

At first reading, these few sentences seem too simple and naive upon which to build a new philosophy and a new religion, but there is far more significance in them than at first appears. And their very simplicity seen over against the background of Hindu philosophy in all its complexity and obscurity, marks them out with the mark of genius. To give a hint, however, of the mine of truth that is here located, let us consider later teachings of Gautama as he developed their implications. To explain what he meant by the 'five groups of clinging,' he analyzes his conception of personality as consisting of body (with unconscious instincts), sensations, perceptions, mental activities, and consciousness; he proves that each of them is transitory, and the clinging they lead to is transitory, and therefore the whole idea of personality is transitory and leads only to suffering. He said in part:

'The body, O Bhikkhus, cannot be the eternal soul, for it tends toward destruction. Nor do sensation, perception, the predispositions and consciousness all together constitute the eternal soul, for were it so, it would not be the case that the consciousness likewise tended toward destruction. Or, how think you, whether form is permanent or transitory? and whether are perception, sensations, predispositions and consciousness permanent or transitory?' 'They are transitory,' replied the five. 'And that which is transitory, is it evil or good?' 'It is evil,' replied the five. 'And that which is transitory, evil and subject to change, can it be said, This is mine, this am I, this is my eternal soul?' 'Nay, verily, it can not be so said,' replied the five. 'Then, O Bhikkhus, it must be said of all physical form whatsoever, past or present or to be, subjective or objective, far or near, high or low, that 'this is not mine, this am I not, this is not my eternal soul."
'And in like manner, of all sensations, perceptions, predispositions and consciousness it must be said, 'This is not mine, this am I not, this is not my eternal soul.' And perceiving this, O Bhikkhus, the true disciple will conceive a disgust for physical form, and for sensations,

perceptions, predispositions and consciousness, and so will be divested of desire; and thereby will be freed and will become aware that he is freed; and he knows that becoming is exhausted, that he has lived the pure life, that he has done what it behooved him to do, that he has put off mortality forever.' —(*Coomaraswamy.*)

The next day a young man by the name of Yasa with fifty-four companions came and listened to him and likewise obtained enlightenment. There were therefore sixty persons besides Gautama, who had obtained enlightenment. These were sent forth to teach and preach. He gave them this great commission:

Go ye, O Bhikkhus, and wander forth for the gain of. the many, for the welfare of the many, out of compassion for the world, for the good, for the gain, for the welfare of gods and men. Proclaim, O Bhikkhus, the doctrine glorious, preach ye a life of holiness, perfect and pure.

Disciples were made with great rapidity. Many of the early ones were educated men already well acquainted with the twists and turns of current and ancient philosophy, but Gautama made no distinctions, he taught and received into membership men of all ranks. This was quite in contrast with the practice of the Brahmin priests, who thought themselves defiled if they exchanged even one word with a low caste man. One day a man of the lowest caste, a sweeper in a temple, listened to him and believed. He was too humble to expect recognition, but Gautama saw by his appearance that he understood, welcomed him into his company with the words, ' Come, O Bhikkhu.' King Pasenadi of the kingdom of Kosala, which included the territory of the Shakyas over which his father was Prince, believed and supported him.

Among these early converts was Uruvela Kassapa, a noted Brahmin scholar, who afterward became his most important disciple. Even down to today in temples where Gautama is worshipped as Buddha, the images of Kassapa and Ananda are placed on either side. One day word was sent to King Bimbisara that Gautama and his company of converts were resting in the King's pleasure park. The King hastened down to meet them, but when he saw Kassapa among them he was at a loss to know which was master and which was disciple. Kassapa saw his perplexity and at once bowed at the feet of Gautama and said, ' The Blessed One is my master; I am his disciple.' Then the King and a great company listened to his words and believed. To show his gratitude the King presented to Gautama the pleasure park called the Bamboo Grove and it became their refuge during the rainy season, and later on the King erected a great monastery there for them.

There was a noted Brahmin ascetic named Sariputta, who was attracted by the noble bearing of one of Gautama's disciples, and inquired of him as to the nature of his master's teachings. The bhikkhu, although he had formerly himself been an ascetic of note, answered humbly,

Brother, I left all things to follow the Shakya sage, that Blessed One is my master and the doctrine I approve is his. Sariputta enquired, ' What then, Venerable Sir, is your teacher's doctrine? ' Brother, replied Assaji, I am a novice and beginner and it is not long that I have retired from the world to adopt his doctrine and discipline, therefore I may set it forth to you in brief, and give the substance of it in few words:

> What things soever are produced by causes
> Of these the Buddha has revealed the cause,
> And likewise how they cease to be;
> This the great Adept proclaims.

Here is expressed in few words the great contribution of Gautama to Indian thought: the eternal continuity of becoming, the denial of a first cause. Sariputta returned to his companion Mogallana, who was equally learned, and together they talked it over; then they went to Gautama, listened to him, were enlightened, and together with Kassapa became his chief disciples.

Meantime word had gone to Prince Suddhodana, the father of Gautama, that his son had obtained enlightenment. The Prince sent messengers to him expressing his desire to see him, but the messengers became so interested in Gautama's teachings that they forgot to return. Finally the Prince sent his minister Kaludayin, who agreed to go only after obtaining permission to join the order if he so desired. The Prince replied, ' Thou mayest become a hermit or not as thou wilt, only bring it about that I see my son.'

Even Kaludayin forgot his message for a full week in his absorption in the Master's words, his own conviction of their truth and the realization of his emancipation. Not until then did he think to deliver the message; Gautama replied that he would go.

Kaludayin hurried back with the reply, but it was two months before Gautama with the great company of followers reached Kapilavathu, his old home. Meanwhile Kaludayin by praising the virtues of Gautama had prepared the way for a favorable reception. They prepared a refuge for the disciples in the Nigroda grove, near the city. As they drew near, the Prince and his ministers and the young men and maidens of the royal family, with flowers in their hands went out to meet them. They led him to the grove, but still thinking him one of themselves, they did not at first show reverence for his person. The Master ignored it and delivered a discourse that so won their respect and awe that beginning with the Prince, his father, they all bowed before him in reverence.

The next day as usual the Master and his followers went early into the city to beg their food. When the citizens saw their prince Siddhattha going from door to door as a mendicant, they looked on in silent amazement. Gautama's wife saw him from a palace window and reported it to the Prince. The Prince instantly went forth and remonstrated with his son for thus putting the Shakya clan to shame. The son replied, ' It is our custom, O King.' The father said, ' Not so, Master, not one of all our ancestors ever begged his bread.' The son replied, ' O King, thy ancestors are all in the succession of kings, but mine are in the succession of Buddhas and they, everyone, have begged their bread and lived on alms.' Then he explained his doctrine to his father more carefully, and did it in so effective a manner that his father almost gained enlightenment then and there, but the full measure of it came a few years later just before his death.

Then the Prince took the Master's begging bowl and led the Blessed One and all his followers to the palace and himself served them with food. After the meal was over the women of the palace came and paid him homage; all but his wife, she remained alone. 'If I have the least value in the eyes of my lord,' she thought, ' he will come to me, then I will do him homage.' So the Blessed One with his two chief disciples went to her chamber and she came to him, and placing her hands on his ankles, laid her face against his feet. The Prince his father said kindly, ' When my daughter heard that thou hadst put on the russet robe, from that time she also dressed in russet garb, and when she heard that thou hadst but one meal a day she took but a single meal, and when she heard that thou hadst forsaken the use of a soft couch she also slept upon a mat on the floor, and when her relatives would have received her and surrounded her with luxuries she did not consider them. Such is her goodness, Blessed One.'

'It is no wonder,' said the Blessed One, 'that she now exercises self control when her wisdom is matured, for she did no less when she was not yet matured.'— (*Coomeraswamy.*)

The next day the Master returned to his former retreat but was followed by a great company of Shakya young men, among whom were his cousins, Ananda, who in his old age became his constant companion and closest intimate, and Devadatta, who through jealousy was always his enemy.

CHAPTER FOUR

THE LIFE OF GAUTAMA, (Concluded)

THE number of the followers of Gautama increased rapidly, and from every rank and caste. Among the notable ones of the early years was Anathapindika, a very wealthy merchant, who gave the Order, as it very early began to be called, a very beautiful park and erected on it a magnificent monastery and then added to his gift a large endowment. There was the Lady Visakha, wife of another rich merchant, who also gave them a monastery second only in splendor to the one given by Anathapindika. She is remembered also for having been able to convert her father-in-law, who had been a prominent member of the rival sect of the Jainas. At another extreme was Bharadvaja, a well known Brahmin, who had charged Gautama and his followers with being parasites; and a fierce bandit named Angulimala; and at still another extreme, there was Ambapali, a beautiful and wealthy courtesan.

But the most important development was in the sixth year of his enlightenment, when women were admitted to the Order. It came about through the death of his beloved father, Prince Suddhodana, who feeling his strength failing

had sent for his son. Gautama dropped everything to go to his father and stayed with him,
comforting him and explaining patiently the
deeper things of his teachings, until his father's
death. After Gautama had returned to his wandering, his step-mother, who had been so much
to him in his childhood, mourning over the death
of her husband and lonely because of the depar-
ture of a favorite son and Gautama's own son
Rahula, who had already joined the Order, decided to try to persuade the Master to let her
join also. With her in this effort were the ladies
of the noble families whose husbands had from
time to time left their homes for the homeless
life of mendicant monks under Gautama. Three
times they were flatly refused on the ground that
it would unnecessarily complicate the situation,
it would perplex the minds of many, would be
the occasion of evil speaking against the Order,
and women could not be depended on to meet the
conditions.

For the fourth time they decided to go to him
with the request. This time they cut their hair,
adopted the same russet garb, took their begging
bowls, and they, who had hitherto hardly walked
an unnecessary step in their lives, went forth
barefooted to walk the many miles to where the
Master was reported to be. Ananda heard of
their coming and went out to meet them. After

hearing their story he returned to Gautama and urged that they be admitted, but was refused. The Master said: ' Enough, Ananda, do not ask me that women retire from the household to a homeless life under our doctrine and discipline '. But Ananda persisted and gradually forced Gautama to admit that women were competent to attain the first stage, the second stage, the third stage and at last he admitted they were competent to reach even ' *Arahatta* ' the first nirvana of enlightenment. Ananda said, ' Are Buddhas born into the world only for the benefit of men? assuredly it is for the benefit of the women also.' This the Master had to admit, but even then he maintained that they could not attain the full Nirvana until they had first been reborn as men. At last Gautama gave his consent, but grudgingly, and he hedged their membership about with additional conditions and requirements, and prophesied that it would be the cause of the earlier decay of the primitive simplicity of the Order.

Gautama was about thirty-five years of age when he obtained enlightenment and he lived after that as a wandering teacher and monk for forty-five years. The area of his wanderings was not extensive, probably less than three hundred miles in any direction, confined to the thickly settled districts about Benares. After the first

flush of his success, the death of his father and
the admission of women to the Order, there followed nearly forty years of varying success.
There were times of hostility and discouragement, it was not all a uniform experience, but
through them all Gautama seems to have preserved the same equanimity, and wise and tactful
behavior. Among these varied experiences may
be mentioned the conversion of Queen Vaidehi,
the wife of his faithful friend King Bimbisara.
She was so proud of her beauty and rank that at
first she disdained to even look upon, much less
meet, the Blessed One. The King however
brought it about by strategy and so tactful and
so winsome were the words of the Master that
she was quickly won over. The means by which
he won her attention was to picture in very
realistic manner one of the beautiful nymphs of
Indra's heaven, and then to quickly portray her
youth, beauty, and power, as they fell into the
decay of old age. Afterward her royal husband
was murdered by their son, and in her very great
sorrow, Gautama came to her and one of the
great scriptures records his words of comfort.
As this scripture afterward became the principal
source of the Amitabha doctrine, it is well to
notice it. It is there written that in his words
of comfort, he varied his usual insistence upon
working out one's own salvation, by telling her

of the surpassing merit of Amitabha's life, who had stored up such a treasure of merit that if anyone in desperate need should claim Amitabha's merit and trust in it, it would be counted as one's own.

At one time some of his leading disciples were challenged to a public exhibition of their powers, but the Master disapproved of it with the wise remark: ' It will neither conduce to the conversion of unbelievers or to the advantage of believers.' Some of his envious opponents conceived the plan of inducing a woman to represent herself to be with child by the Master. When brought to his presence he listened to her story and then said kindly, ' Sister, whether your words be true or false you and I best know.' He provided a place and care for her until his innocence was proven to all.

There was a serious dispute among the disciples about certain rules of discipline, which led the Master to withdraw by himself, but later they decided among themselves to refer it to the Master and to abide by his decision. For a time the Master was subjected to violent insults by his father-in-law but he bore them patiently. And for many years he was made very unhappy by the envy of his cousin Devadatta, who while remaining in the Order sought in malignant ways to undermine Gautama's authority and influence, and to promote his own advancement. At last the Master had to expel him from the Order. Davadatta went to the crown prince of King Bimbisara and persuaded him to kill the King and usurp his authority, while he himself brought about the death of Gautama and made himself master of the Order. The first part was carried out, but the men sent to kill the Master were themselves converted. Then Devadatta sought to create a schism in the order but failed, was sick a long time and then in weakness of body sought to re-enter the Order but failed and later died in some great agony.

In the midst of this awful strain a quarrel broke out between the new king of Kosala and the Shakyas. Pressure was brought to bear on Gautama to side with his family in their troubles but he refused, and in the war which followed the Shakyas were well nigh exterminated, and of the aggressors, the Kosalas, many perished soon after in an unprecedented flood.

When the Master was seventy-nine, he was urged to interfere in another war, as one of the parties was friendly to his teachings. Again he refused, but encouraged his friends by saying that as long as they were faithful to his teachings they need have no fear. Following this the Master called together the prominent men of the Order and set before them forty-one conditions

KWANNON

This image, the so-called Goddess of Mercy, represents an incarnation just below the rank of Buddha, of the Divine mercy and compassion. She is the hearer and answerer of all prayer. The vial is symbolic of the ambrosia of forgiveness; she is the Holy Spirit of Divine Love.

It is a modern copy in bronze of a very ancient Korean original, 27½ inches over all. It is now in the Author's collection.

AMIDA BUDDHA

This represents the theistic and personalized form of Buddahood that is characteristic of the Shin-shu Sect, that believe in Salvation through Faith in Amida's Great Vow, by the single repetition of the phrase: Namu Amida Butzu (I adore Thee and claim thy merits, O Amida, Lord of Life and Light and Love).

The figure is 19 inches high, 36 inches over all. It is made of wood exquisitely carved and is covered with red and gold lacquer. It was made by an artist of the Mimoto school, of the early Tokagawa era, about 1700 A. D., and came from a temple in Yamato, near Nara. It is now in the Author's collection.

for their kind of *warfare*. Some of these had to
do with laymen as well as monks, but among
those that were for the monks especially are the
following regulations, which are as applicable as
ever:

So long, O Bhikkhus, ... as the brethren delight
in a life of solitude . . . . shall not be engaged in, be
fond of, or be connected with business . . . . shall not
stop on their way to Nirvana because they have attained
to any lesser thing . . . . shall exercise themselves in
mutual activity, search after truth, energy, joy, peace,
earnest contemplation, and equanimity of mind, ...
shall exercise themselves in the realization of the ideas of
the impermanency of all phenomena, bodily and mental,
. . . . in the practice, both in public and in private, of
those virtues that are productive of freedom and praised
by the wise, and are untarnished by desire of a future
life, or the faith in the efficacy of outward acts . . . .
shall live cherishing, both in public and private, that
noble and saving insight which leads to the complete destruction of the sorrow of him who acts according to it,
so long may the brethren be expected not to decline but
to prosper. . . . . Such and such is upright conduct;
such and such is earnest contemplation, such and such is
intelligence. Great becomes the fruit, great the advantage of intellect when it is set round with earnest contemplation. The mind set round with intelligence is set
quite free from the intoxications, that is from the intoxication of sensuality, from the intoxication of becoming,
from the intoxication of delusion of selfhood, from the
intoxication of ignorance.

As the eightieth year of the Master's life drew
on he seemed eager to visit familiar scenes. The
last rainy season was spent at the shelter in
Beluva. There a severe sickness came on him,

but feeling that his time had not yet come, he combatted it with all his might and it abated. When he had recovered Ananda asked him if he had any instructions as to what should be done by the Order, or who should lead it, after he was gone. This is his reply.

. . . . Surely, Ananda, should there be anyone who harbors the thought, ' It is I, who will lead the brotherhood,' or ' The Order is dependent upon me,' it is he who should lay down instructions in any matter concerning the Order. Now the Tathagata thinks not that it is he who should lead the brotherhood, or that the Order is dependent on him. Why then should he leave instructions in any matter concerning the Order? I too, O Ananda, am now grown old and full of years, my journey is drawing to a close, I have reached the sum of days, I am turning eighty years of age; and just as a wornout cart, Ananda, can be kept going only with the help of thongs so, methinks, the body of the Tathagata can only be kept going by bandaging it up. It is only, Ananda, when the Tathagata, by ceasing to attend to any outward thing, becomes plunged by the cessation of any separate sensation into that concentration of heart which is concerned with no material object, it is only then that the body of the Tathagata is at ease.

Therefore, O Ananda, be ye lamps unto yourselves. Be ye a refuge unto yourselves. Betake yourselves to no external refuge. Hold fast to the Truth as a lamp. Hold fast as a refuge to the Truth. Look not for a refuge to any one besides yourselves. . . . . And whosoever, Ananda, either now or after I am dead, shall be a lamp to themselves, shall betake themselves to no external refuge, but holding fast to the Truth as their lamp, and holding fast as their refuge to the Truth, shall look not for refuge to anyone beside themselves—it is they, Ananda, among my Bhikkhus, who shall reach the topmost height. But even they must be anxious to learn.— (*Translation by Coomeraswamy.*)

When the sunny days came again, they journeyed on to Kutagara Hall in the Great Forest and there many of the brothers assembled. The Blessed One made announcement of his coming death: ' Behold now, O brethren, I exhort you, saying, All component things must grow old. Work out your salvation with diligence. The final extinction of the Tathagata will take place before long. At the end of three months the Tathagata will die.'

They moved to Para and they rested in the mango grove of Cunda, a blacksmith, who invited the Master to dine at his house. The food offered was mushrooms and soon after he fell deadly sick; probably some poisonous variety had been included carelessly. He bore it without complaint and went on with his speaking. After the worst had passed they travelled on to Kusinara. There The Blessed One asked Ananda to spread his robe, saying, ' I am weary, Ananda, I must rest awhile.'

Then they moved across the river Kaputtha and the Blessed One requested them to send back a messenger to Cunda, the blacksmith, telling him that the Tathagata in no wise blamed him for the error which had caused his sickness. He said, ' *Tell him there are two meals which have been very precious to me: the one Sujita gave me just before my enlightenment, and the one he*

*gave me just before my final passing away.   Let
him feel no remorse.*'

They slowly moved on to the Sala Grove of the
Mallas on the further side of the river Hiranya-
vati. He again asked Ananda to spread his robe
as he was very tired, but he continued conscious
and self-possessed. The legends say there were
many marvels took place: although it was out
of season the Sala trees broke out into full bloom
and there was heavenly music. The Blessed One
spoke of seeing a vision of heavenly beings.
When Ananda retired to relieve his overcharged
heart of its sorrow, the Blessed One noticed it,
sent for him and comforted him. He also thought
to send a messenger to the neighboring village to
tell them that the Tathagata was to spend the
night near them, so that afterwards they would
not be disappointed at not having welcomed him
to their vicinity.

He asked the brethren if any had any doubts
about his teachings, and when no one admitted
of doubt he spoke of his utmost faith in them.
He explained some of the more obscure points of
his teachings ending with the words, ' Decay is
inherent in all component things; work out your
salvation with diligence.' These were his last
words.

The body was held until the arrival of Kassapa
and other leading followers and was then cre-

mated. The unconsumed bones and ashes were divided into eight parts and distributed among the Ajatasatta, Vesali, his kinsmen the Shakyas, Alakappa, Ramagama, the Brahmin of Vethadipa, and the Mallas of Kusinara where he had died. These portions were buried and later at different times costly monuments were erected over them. Only a few years ago a mound of decayed brick and overgrown with shrubs, near the birthplace of Gautama, was examined. Within there was discovered a stone vault in which there were several crystal vases filled with ornaments of gold and jewels; the most beautiful of the crystal vases contained pieces of charred bones and ashes and was engraved, ' This is the receptacle for the relics of the sublime Buddha, a pius offering of the Shakyas, the brothers and sisters and their sons and wives.' These are now in the Calcutta Museum.

To this day flowers are laid before the statues of the Buddha, not as sacrifices to a god, but to show the esteem and veneration felt for him as the best and wisest of men, who never can be sufficiently venerated for having given his doctrine to the world. The formula used on these occasions is:

' He is the Sublime One, the Master, the perfectly Enlightened One, The Perfect One in knowledge and deeds, the Blessed One, the Knower of worlds, the Incomparable One, the Leader of erring humanity, the Teacher of gods and men, the Buddha.'

CHAPTER FIVE

THE TEACHINGS OF GAUTAMA

THE Enlightenment of Gautama consisted in the recognition of certain fundamental truths which became indelibly fixed in his mind by vision and ecstasy. This experience and conviction, he taught, was open and available to all who would follow his way of life. His teachings were not all new, of course, some he had received through his early Brahmin tutors from the ancient Vedic teachings and the then modern Upanishads; some were from his studies and experience with Udakka, the Yoga ascetic; and some were from Alara Kalama, the Sankhaya ascetic; but in the crucible of his mind they took on new meanings and new relations until the system as a whole was quite original.

Gautama, believing that the human intellect shared the imperfections and the limits of the impermanent body, taught and practised a very modest and tolerant agnosticism. Certain things we might know, like rules of life based on experience, but other things, like the existence and nature of the gods, the existence and the nature of the conscious soul after the death of the body, the nature of the ultimate ' Void,' were unknowable and therefore inconsequential to one's well being and peace of mind. Gautama, therefore, avoided the discussion of all metaphysical and speculative questions.

As he did not believe that one could know anything about a supreme and a transcendent God or a life after death, he is frequently charged with being an atheist and an agnostic. As Christians have often misunderstood the extent of Gautama's agnosticism and atheism, it is well to make it perfectly clear in the beginning, that his teachings were not necessarily atheistic, or his religion, in a true sense, pessimistic. We must recall and keep clearly in mind that Gautama had a background of excessive speculation, polytheism and egoism, against which he had reacted. That which made Buddhism at first distinctive was its ' *this worldliness.*' But he did not out and out reject the metaphysical teachings of his day, he only held that one could not come to any positive conclusion concerning them and therefore any disputation about them would not lead to that quiet frame of mind which is essential to the attainment of Nirvana.

To make clear his position, which is characteristic of all early Buddhism, let us take two instances. On one occasion in a discussion with a Brahmin, he had said that he did not hold one view or the opposite.

The Brahmin said, 'Has then the Ascetic Gautama no views at all?' The Buddha replied, 'These views the Tathagata has surpassed. But he knows, Thus is the bodily form, thus it originates, thus it passes away. . . . The Tathagata is liberated having given up all clinging; because for him all imaginings, all suppositions, all ideas relating to self and mine have disappeared, are gone, annulled, abolished, rooted out.' Not yet satisfied the Brahmin asked, 'Where does such a liberated being reappear?' 'It reappears is not correct.' 'Then it does not reappear?' 'It does not reappear is not correct.' — (*Straus.*)

Do not think by this that Gautama was incapable of deep and logical reasoning. If you harbor such a thought as that read his teaching concerning the universality of suffering, or the doctrine of anatta, non-selfness. But Gautama was wise enough not to waste time arguing about things that were essentially unknowable. Gautama had a better access to truth than disputation, namely, follow the Eightfold Path which will lead to an immediate awareness of the highest wisdom.

When he was directly asked by an ascetic of another school whether there exists an independent soul or not, he remained silent. Later on one of his disciples asked him why he did not answer. He said, 'If I had replied, yes, to his question, is there a self? I should have approved those who teach the immortality of the soul. Had I answered, no, I should have approved those who teach absolute annihilation in death. This is one of the questions that do not lead to quietness, to real knowledge, to enlightenment, to Nirvana; it lies beyond our power of discernment, and those who assert the one as well as those who assert the other, assert something which they cannot know.' — (*Straus.*)

Indian thought had focussed on the doctrine of the Atman, the Universal Self. In contrast, Gautama focussed his thought on the doctrine of Anatta, the not-self. He held that we can only know what the Essential Self is not. We may not know the nature of the innermost principle of things for that is inconceivable. By following the true way of life we may become aware, by intuitive insight, that there is a blissful splendor within, but just what it is we may not know.

While Gautama deprecated speculation as to what the Essential Self may be, he urged his disciples to follow the Golden Path, which would bring them at the long last to its endless, shoreless, spirituality. There would be an end of thirst, of clinging, of suffering; seeing no more pictures, thinking no more thoughts; there would be no more ego nor object, neither withinness nor withoutness, simply no-thing.

Now, Patthapada, it may be that you are thinking, 'Defilement certainly may vanish, purity may increase, and here on earth one may see the fulness and perfect unfolding of wisdom through one's own knowledge, and attain to enduring possession thereof, but that must be a very dreary life.' But the matter is not thus to be regarded, Patthapada; rather will all that I have mentioned happen, and then only joy, pleasure, quietude, earnest reflection, complete consciousness and bliss ensue. —(*Translation by Grimm.*)

To the mental eye there is only boundless space and nothingness, but in its sublime solitude there is an indescribable Peace and Blessedness, to which one who has experienced it ever turns from the tormenting thirst and turmoil of the earthly life.

' How can there be bliss, where there is no sensation? ' an enquirer asks of Sariputta. Sariputta replies: ' This, precisely, O friend, is bliss, that here there is no sensation. '

But Gautama taught that there were certain intimations of what is above and beyond which are revealed by the sane use of our senses, mental processes and intuitive faculties, which can be checked up by the experience of each disciple. Among these is the universal presence in nature of an endless process of change and becoming that is characterized by two aspects: an inviolable sequence of cause and effect that appears in physics as the conservation of energy, in animate life as heredity and evolution, in morals as retribution, in thought as logic. It ever tends toward new form, new combinations, rebirth. It is the creative power of thought; it is *the must be* of Truth. But as it acts blindly, inevitably, it is of the nature of *ignorance*.

This endless process of change and becoming has also another aspect. It seems to move toward some good end, it is benevolent in that it co-operates in the direction of freer adaptation, increase of mutual participation, clearer awareness, enlightenment and a deepening sense of identity and blissful peace. In other words, back of this endless process of change and becoming is an immanent Principle to which everything must conform, a Principle which is characterized by the interweaving and blending in endlessly varying proportion of two qualities: Karma, Truth, and Karuna, Love.

This process while having its cycles and rhythms and limits, apparently has no precise point of beginning or absolute ending. What appear as such like the origin of atoms and the attainment of Nirvana are but stages in its progress. Viewed from the human standpoint, the blind energy of the atomic world seems the extreme of ignorance, the very polar opposite of the loving intelligence, sympathy, kindness, unity of the Bodhicitta at the other pole. But all the time there is only one All-inclusive, everywhere Immanent Dharmakaya which is both Principle of Love and substance of Truth blending into one undifferentiated harmonious Whole. Nirvana is the passing from Karmic determinism and particularity into identity with the Buddhahood which is the serene and blissful peace of Love's All-inclusiveness. But Bodhicitta, the Heart of Loving Intelligence, is also Dharmakaya, the Womb of Truth, from whose unfailing fountain flows endlessly the radiant, vibrating energy of the atomic world.

In this vast Process of Becoming, everything is an expression of the Dharmakaya, not as ex-

ternal to Itself but as rhythms within Itself.
Thought, energy, matter, life, consciousness,
ideas, spirit, all are transient appearances of one
Essential Reality, namely, the Dharmakaya.
All these appearances are subject to Karma and
are conditioned by Karuna, and everything is in
gradual progress toward unification, not by adding something on, not by some external compulsion, but by its own inherent nature, by a gradual
unwrapping, exfoliation, getting rid of, the bonds
and impediments of *ignorance.*

The human body with its unified consciousness,
which we call, the soul or the ego or the I, is
only one of these innumerable, finite and transient appearances. With the death of the body,
the soul also ceases to be. But back of its appearance on the physical plane there is a corresponding *living idea* on the psychic plane which
has been developing along with it and which per-
sists after the appearance has vanished. This
living idea immediately tends to express itself
anew in a more adequate appearance on the physical plane. In time after many rebirths as conditioned by its Karma, an adequate expression
of the *idea* can no longer be made under the
physical conditions of human life, and thereafter
its rebirths must necessarily be under the freer
conditions of the Psychic Realm, the Pure Land
of the Arahats. Still under its Karmic law, this

idea will then unfold in the Psychic Realm until its further expression can only adequately be made under the freer and more inclusive conditions of the Spiritual Realm, as *significance,* as a Bodhisattva. And in the long last the Bodhisattva will achieve his Nirvana, full identity with the Buddhahood, free at last of all limiting and entangling ignorance and particularity. Herein all distinctions of subject and object, male and female, thought and thinker, are merged in the blissful unity of the Bodhicitta, the Intelligence Heart, wherein Love and Truth are merged in the pure consciousness of an all-inclusive sympathy and compassion.

> For they (Bodhisattvas) consider all sentient beings as their own self and do not cling to their individual forms. How is this? Because they know truthfully that all sentient beings as their own self come from one and the same *Suchness,* and no distinction can be established among them.—(*Suzuki's translation of Ashvaghosha.*)

Any idea of selfhood, of I or mine, is therefore an illusion of ignorance that must be gotten rid of.

Gautama goes to great length to prove beyond all dispute that the clinging to selfness is clinging to something that vanishes at death. He does not deny that personality has an essence that is eternal, but he insists that the body, its sensations, its perceptions, its consciousness, its thinking, is not of that essence. So long as a man clings to the idea that the *conscious* I has an independent value that is eternal, he fears suffering, death and annihilation, but when he appreciates that consciousness, as well as body, is alien to his essential nature, he becomes perfectly indifferent to them. Gautama says: ' Just even so, ye monks, what is not yours surrender. Long will its surrender make for your happiness and well-being. And what is it that is not yours? Body, monks, is not yours; sensation is not yours; the activities of the mind are not yours; consciousness is not yours. Give them up, one and all. Long will their giving up tend to your happiness and well-being.'

What is the essential self, then? Gautama says we may know what it is not; what it is we may never know, it is inscrutable. We may know that the essential self is not a part of the evanescent world and its process. At death all else is annihilated, save only the essential self, that is not annihilated because it is not a part of it; it is alien to it.

Although the idea of an independent selfhood as an immortal entity is an illusion, nevertheless, being subject in its birth and death to the universal law of cause and effect, the true self does persist and appears and reappears in rebirths that are conditioned by a parallel growth of *idea* in the psychic plane just above. This conditioning or causative influence, Karma, is conceived of as the reservoir or storage of the desires and behavior and acts of each successive rebirth in its series. That is, there is action and reaction between these different planes of existence; for instance, Karma is the record of the acts of each particular organism, and is ever varying as these acts affect its record; but it is also ever seeking to express its record in new and corresponding form and surroundings and rebirth, on this or some other plane of reality.

This karmic record can, by the suitable acts and desires of the organism, *burn itself out;* the soul is then said to have obtained its enlightenment. That is, the karmic record has reached a point where it is exempt from the old necessity of rebirth into the pain and suffering of the physical life. That is, while the body may still be functioning on the physical plane, its truer self is functioning on the psychical plane as an arahat or saint, or deva. This stage is sometimes also called nirvana, but it is different from the real Nirvana. The first nirvana is the point where the appearance-body passes into bliss-body; the real Nirvana is the point where the bliss-body gives way to the essence-body of the Dharmakaya. The first nirvana of enlightenment only releases the soul from certain chains of ignorance, namely from the illusion and in-

toxication of the lust of the senses, the illusions
and infatuations of the mental processes (understood not as an absence of learning and experience, but as delusions that have been accumu-
lated from past births and experiences, and
which effectually separate the soul from its essential self, which is Buddhahood), and from the
illusion and obsession of independent selfhood.

While the enlightened soul in its human existence already enjoys some of the blessings of a
higher life, such as a less hampered view of truth
and reality, and a relative immuneness to the
illusions and thirsts of the mortal life, it does
not at the death of the body pass as a continuation of the conscious soul into the higher life
of the psychic realm. It is the essential Buddha-
nature that is immanent in him, that now finds
a new and different expression in the further
rebirths still under its karmic determinism but
under the freer and happier conditions of a
higher level of cosmic life, first as *idea* and afterward on the spiritual plane as *pure significance.*

In the process from the atomic world through
the stage of conscious human life to the Bodhicitta and the Dharmakaya, Gautama discerned
several stages or planes of existence, that are not
mutually exclusive but are relative and interweaving, the one shading into the other. He
thought of them in ' personal ' terms, but it is

well to carry in mind the corresponding scientific terms.

1. The world of 'hungry demons'; the world of matter and 'ignorance'; (the atomic realm of blind energy).

2. The world of Demons; (the plane of protoplasmic and bacterial life).

3. The Sensitive plane of ghosts (vegetation).

4. The Perceptive world of animal life.

5. The Conscious world of human life.

6. The Deva world of angelic life; the world of 'name and form'; (the plane of 'living ideas,' the psychic realm). Existence on this plane is relatively free of space, but still subject to birth, growth, and inclusion into more general concepts. It is the Pure Land of the Arahats.

7. The Spiritual Realm; entirely free of 'name and form,' relatively free of time, particularity and definition, but still embodying distinctions among universals, such as *significance,* wisdom, truth, compassion, love and equanimity, bliss and peace. It is the realm of the Bodhisattvas; beyond is the undifferentiated, inconceivable unity and harmony of the Bodhicitta and Dharmakaya.

Gautama was more concerned in making clear an analysis of those more immediate and tangible influences that conditioned the good life and in mapping out the necessary steps for living it and attaining enlightenment and Nirvana. He enunciated the following chain of causation, which is known as the Twelve Nirdanas:

1. From ignorance (*avijja*) arises phenomena (*sankhara*). 2. From phenomena arises the principle of life (*vinnana*). 3. From life arises living organisms (*nama-rupa*). 4. From living organism arises the six senses (*salayatana*). 5. From the six senses arises contact (*phassa*). 6. From contact arises sensation, etc. (*vedana*). 7. From sensation arises thirst (*tanha*). 8. From thirst arises grasping (*upadana*). 9. From grasping arises "becoming" (*bhava*). 10. From "becoming" arises birth (*jata*). 11. From birth arises sickness, old age, disappointment, sorrow, pain and death. 12. From suffering arises a thirst for the illusion of a life free from suffering, that is for rebirth in a new nama-rupa (3), and so on indefinitely.

Meditation on this led Gautama to pronounce the Four Noble Truths.

1. The fact of suffering: everything has a cause and leads to suffering.

2. Suffering arises from the thirst and consequent grasping after (a) the illusions of the bodily senses; (b) the illusions of the mental processes; (c) the illusions of "selfness."

3. Suffering ceases when these thirsts can be eradicated.

4. The way to get rid of thirst, and therefore of its consequent grasping after its illusions, is to follow the Golden Eightfold Path.

This Golden Path is the Way of Salvation for all Buddhists; it brings release from the thirsts of attachment, the fears of rebirths; the attainment of enlightenment, spiritual insight and blissful peace, and the assurance of final identification with the Buddhahood.

The First Step is Right Views of Life: the acceptance of the Four Noble Truths.

Second, Right Aspiration. To follow the Path one must, first of all, really want to attain enlightment and Nirvana; there must be a determination to follow the path and stick to it to the end; there must be the renunciation of all pride or confidence in one's conscious selfhood, the resolution to live in right relations with all animate life, not to harbor ill-will, or cause suffering, and the renunciation of all covetousness and avarice and impurity.

Third, Right Speech. This means abstaining from all lying, slander, false witness, abuse, boasting and idle talk. It is written, ' Two things are suitable for a Buddhist, edifying conversation and wise silence.'

Fourth, Right Action. Abstaining from the taking of any life and from any unkindness whatever, abstaining from stealing or the taking of any thing whatever that is not freely given, abstaining from adultery or any unchaste act or thought. It is noticeable that Buddhist ethics appear to lay greater emphasis on abstaining from unkind and unchaste acts than upon the encouragement to do kind acts.

Fifth, Right Livelihood. This naturally follows from the preceding, one must avoid any calling that involves unkindness, deceit, or impurity. No Buddhist could engage in butchering for the market, running a sweat shop, being a soldier, or an exploiter of others' labor, or marketing impure foods, or intoxicating drinks, and, of course, avoiding any calling that appealed to the passions, like gambling or prostitution.

Sixth, Right Effort. One must constantly seek to suppress the appearance of evil states of mind, laziness, lust or anger; and stimulate good states of mind and conserve and perfect all wise and kind impulses. This heading is often elaborated in the sutras by advising in detail as to ways and means of attaining the end. Buddhists consider this step important because it is the crowning act of the physical life and prepares the way and leads up to life on the psychic plane which is covered by the Seventh and thence to life on the spiritual plane which is covered by the Eighth.

Seventh, Right Meditation. If the previous steps have been carefully taken the believer is supposed to be free from clinging and illusion. Now he is to do those things which will keep his mind free, ardent, self-possessed, serene and thoughtful. He must spend much time in meditation. Christians have always placed much emphasis, almost an exclusive emphasis, on thoughtfulness as logical reasoning. The Buddhists' scholars are no less logical, but they place the emphasis, not on reasoning itself or the result of reasoning, but on thoughtful meditation on the conclusions to which their reasoning has brought them. Gautama recognized that the mind included memory with all its unconscious predilections and habits and desires which must all be censored by the conscious mind; it included the perceptive faculties with all their untrust-worthy tendencies; it included the reasoning mind which grouped, discriminated, and selected to pragmatic ends; it included the intellect with all its dangers of rationalizing and false premises and mistaken conclusions; and the imagination and fancy with their captivating allurements; he recognized that it was by meditation only that the sure approach to truth and reality was to be made. But most important of all meditation served by quietly focussing the mind on some good truth to prepare it for a further and still more valuable attainment.

Eighth, Right Concentration. Sometimes this is translated, Right Rapture. Not only has the mind of man an intellect, he has also intuitive faculties by which he may pass beyond the con-tacts of experience and reasoning into an im-mediacy of awareness. To gain the fruits of intuition, the thinking mind must not only be free from distractions but focussed to its finest. He must then rise above thought into an identity with reality which will bring both unshakable conviction and unspeakable rapture. If successful it undoubtedly leads to trance and ecstasy, to a kind of self-hypnotism, in which the spirit is entirely freed from its bonds of illusion. When the intellect is at its best in quiet meditation, the heart often hungers and longs for something beyond. The intellect may tire and abandon its search for truth, but the heart never abandons its longing for love, and once having experienced the beatific vision is forever satisfied; with the vision and the ecstasy comes an enhancement of life that later suffering can never eradicate or dim, and a peaceful equanimity that troubles can never disturb.

Enlightenment might come with the Seventh Step, or with the Sixth, and with it would come the first nirvana, or passing out of the entanglements of the physical life into correspondence with the freer conditions of the psychic process.

The successful attainment of the Eighth Step is but an anticipation of what will be the commonplace when the 'spark' of the Buddhahood which is in every animate life is finally freed of its impending bonds of 'ignorance' and finds itself one with the Bodhicitta, the Heart of Wisdom.

Honestly following the Golden Path brings one to successive stages in the life process, namely,

1. The first and second steps will end the old ignorant and aimless wandering and bring a certain peace of mind.

2. The third, fourth, and fifth steps will bring the gradual decrease and ending of the thirst arising from the five senses and the consequent clinging to them.

3. The sixth step will bring the gradual decrease and ending of the thirst arising from the mental processes, and the consequent clinging to the illusions of the mind, pride of intellect, etc.

4. Also, it will bring the gradual decrease of the thirst of the conscious mind for its illusions of 'selfness,' its thirsts for larger self-realization and self-glorification and for conscious survival after the death of the body and for an eternal life.

5. The attainment of increased wisdom and spiritual insight, peace of mind and quiet happiness, namely, 'the ten graces.'

6. The fruit of the Seventh Step — Right Meditation — are the Four Absorptions, namely,

   a. Spiritual Insight: one no longer thinks of suffering and pain and self.

   b. Joy and Happiness incident to this release.

c. Equanimity of mind: riddance even of the thought of the above joy and happiness.

d. The Blissful Peace that follows the fading out of all past joys and sorrows, 'in the painless, pleasureless purity of an even and concentrated mind.'

7. With this Blissful Peace, which is the highest reach of the self-conscious mind, comes the state of Enlightenment, which is the first nirvana; henceforth there will be no more re-births on the physical plane: they will have become Arahats, Enlightened Ones.

8. The fruits of the Eighth Step — Right Concentration — are the Four Holy States, namely,

a. The General State of Blissful Peace.

b. The Gracious Radiation of Compassion.

c. The Gracious Radiation of Sympathetic Gladness.

d. The Gracious Radiation of Perfect Equanimity.

9. Nirvana: the extinction of all rebirths, all self-consciousness, and all ' particularity.'

10. The full attainment of the ' pure' consciousness of identity with the Buddahood, which is the Dharmakaya, the superessential Selfhood of the Unified Whole.

Some scholars will be inclined to question the inclusion of the conception of Bodhisattvas in the teachings of Gautama, limiting the primative teachings to The Four Noble Truths, the Chain of Causation, The Golden Path, Enlightenment, Arhats, Non-permanent-soul and Nirvana; but the writer feels confident that much more was included, in embryo at least. Gautama's well known habit of reticence in regard to the deeper metaphysical implications in his teachings prevented any extended reference or elucidation to many things he must have discussed with his more scholarly followers like Maha-Kasyapa and Sariputta, who were well versed in these very subtleties. Moreover all the Amida sects who make much of the Bodhisattva conception trace their fundamental tenets to seed thoughts of Gautama himself in the earliest of the Agama literature and the Jataka birth stories.

Gautama solved the practical problem of getting rid of suffering and advancing into a higher life-process, not by dialectics that must be accepted on authority, but by direct experience in such a manner that everyone, by his own experience, perception and immediate insight may convince himself of the correctness of the solution, and at any time when he wishes to do so, may retest it upon himself. Gautama held fast to this one practical rule of life and preached it in season and out: suffering, its cause and cure, and the path to its cessation. 'Following my instructions, ye shall know and realize that utmost noble goal of the holy life, for yourselves even in this present life.' 'Whether the dogma obtains that the world is eternal or is not eternal, there still remain birth, old age, death, sorrow and lamentation, misery, grief and despair, for the extinction of which in the present life, I am prescribing.'

Gautama warns against all belief except personal insight gained by following the Eightfold Path. He asks only one thing of his disciples: the personal treading of the way shown him, by which he may win for himself the intuitive apprehension of truth. Follow his map and the stations will successively appear, one by one.

Not directly at the beginning will certainty be obtained, but gradually striving, gradually struggling, striding on pace by pace, certainty is at last attained . . . .. A man of trust comes near, having come near he associates . . . he listens . . . he hears the teaching . . . he retains it . . . . he contemplates the meaning . . . . it gives him insight . . . he approves it . . . . he puts it into practice . . . . he realizes in his own person the supreme truth . . . . he is brought face to face with reality.— (*Adapted from George Grimm's the Doctrine of the Buddha.*)

Gautama offers to lead not the exceptional man, but 'the honest, straightforward man,' by a quite definite mode of training up the mountain of pure cognition. 'Below he will see for himself the billowing fog of earth's suffering, above and all about he will see a delectable land, a serene garden, a magnificent forest, a landscape all abloom, a bright pool of water.' Nor from this height need he ever return to the valley.

With this vantage comes an insight and wisdom that is unhampered and unclouded by any kind of illusion, or desire, or clinging. But this is still not the end. After spiritual insight and heavenly wisdom follows an ineffable love for all things without distinction. Concerning this love, Gautama says, 'All means in this life for the earning of merit are not worth one-sixteenth part of love which is deliverance from the mind. Love, the deliverance of the mind, takes them up into itself, shining and glowing and beaming.' Its glory and graciousness floods through the believer in such an immeasurable stream that it knows no bounds, no dimunition. There will be no hiding of secret reservations, there only will be the simplest, most unsullied loving kindness and compassion and equanimity, never ending, unfolding, expanding and enveloping. 'Thus, my monks, must you train yourselves,' said Gautama.

There were two grades of believers: the laity and the monks and nuns. The Master gave the laity only five rules: they must avoid destruction

of life, which was interpreted to include all unkindness, as well as killing, to all animate life,
and hence they could eat no meat. They must
avoid theft, adultery, lying and the use of intoxicating drinks.

For the monks and nuns there were five more,
namely: they must avoid eating between meals,
which was often interpreted to mean eating only
one meal a day, or at most two, and nothing after
noon; they must avoid attendance at any secular
entertainment or social affair; they must omit
the use or possession of ointments and jewelry;
the use of 'high' or soft beds, and the handling
of money. For the monks and nuns the third
rule concerning adultery included the avoidance
of all sex indulgence and unchastity of any kind
in thought or behavior. As the years went by,
to meet particular situations, the Master established other regulations, adding to them from
time to time until there were some 250 for the
monks and some 300 for the nuns. Practically
all of these rules were taken over from existing
rules among other mendicant orders; later on
other rules applying to the laity were added
which were current among the Brahmin and had
to do with a blameless life, particularly as to
kindness to animals, respect toward parents, and
the giving of alms to the brethren.

Among these rules for the monks were such

regulations as forbade ownership of property, the carrying of extra or expensive clothing, or shoes, or surplus food. They were to beg for their daily food and sleep where night found them, within their own monasteries, or if invited, in houses, otherwise under a shed or tree. They were not to start public speaking, but if asked questions by the people they met or were asked to speak, they were to give their time freely in kindly and tolerant explanation of the teachings of the Blessed One or of their own ideas relating thereto.

While the practice of good works is not especially enjoined, except under the general head of kindness, yet from the very beginning we find the brethren active in teaching both young and old, and fostering all manner of good works. After the Master's death, wherever the institution of monasticism became established, Buddhism contributed effectively toward raising the general standard of social ethics, education and good works.

When the rainy season set in the brethren gathered at their shelters and monasteries and there, if the Master was present, laid before him their troubles and experiences, told him their temptations and failures and received his kindly counsel and sympathy. Later this 'confession' became a regular occurrence and, if the Master was not present, they confessed to each other in a general meeting and were often admonished but seldom punished, except in rare cases when they were dropped from membership; later on they were often reinstated. During these seasons those less adept in meditation or scholarship, were taught by the more able ones, but there was no compulsion about it. All, from highest to lowest, wore the same cheap or cast off clothing, ate the same simple vegetable food, and slept on the same mats spread on flat boards or on the floor. There was no government as such but the general influence of the brothers. The control within the Buddhist monasteries from the beginning has been quite democratic, a selection by common consent of an abbot who appoints to the other positions of direction and administration. Sometimes there are frequent changes, the retired abbots forming a kind of unofficial advisers, but they receive no extras.

From the very beginning, also, there developed a deep love for nature and its solitudes. The forest hermitage was seen to be more conducive to meditation and the restraint of desire, than were the crowded streets. There are many tender, sweet poems indicating this.

> Who doth not love to see on either bank
> Clustered rose-apple trees in fair array,
> Beyond the great cave of the hermitage,
> Or hear the soft croak of the frogs?

When in the lowering sky thunders the storm cloud's drum,
And all the pathways of the birds are thick with rain,
A brother sits within the hollow of the hills
Alone, rapt in thought's ecstasy.   No higher bliss
Is given to men than this.
                              —(*Psalms of the Brothers.*)

    In golden light on the sun-kissed peaks,
    The water, murmuring in the pebbly creeks,
    Are Buddha. In silence, hark, he speaks.
                              —(*Unknown*)

        My bamboo hut is low and tiny
        I sit alone; it is in spring;
        My flowers bloom in rare profusion;
        The breeze is soft the south wind brings.
        But yester eve my friend had promised
        To see my garden blooming fair:
        I sit alone today, but listen
        To gentle rain and free from care.
        —(*Soyen Shaku, trans. by B. L. Suzuki.*)

Buddhists are far from being a sad or discouraged people; on the contrary, they are
notably cheerful and happy. A Christian minister once said of his people that they took their
religion soberly but not seriously. The Buddhists take their religion seriously and cheerfully.
When one becomes accustomed to the thought
that life is impermanent, but, brief as it is, that
it is an expression of the Buddha nature, and that
the way is open toward the Pure Land and
Nirvana, and that any advance that is made is
so much gained, that, in the long last, we and
all animate life will participate in the Buddhahood, there comes a feeling of deep content that

all is well. Moreover the Buddhist life is not a selfish life. Gautama made it very emphatic and clear that while our conscious mind could know nothing of an eternal life, yet nevertheless, their desires and behavior and effort conditioned the rebirths under their Karma, so that, while there would be no conscious future life for them personally, the lives of innumerable others yet to be born under their Karma, would be made easier and happier.

CHAPTER SIX

BUDDHISM TO THE TIMES OF KING ASOKA

AFTER the mourning over the death of Gautama was somewhat allayed the brethren came together to discuss their future. One of the things that they did was to write down some of the important discourses of the Master. It is recorded that 'Upali, the barber,' was chosen to repeat the most important, and Ananda another. Some authorities assert that the sutras were not written down for two hundred years, but this seems improbable when we recall that writing was in common use at that time in Assyria, Greece, Egypt and China. There seems to be no reason why India with all her interests in learning and with all her wealth and political power should not have been acquainted with the art also. That the use of writing was limited to a few persons and to the most important matters may be readily admitted. The result of this first Council was the first canon of scriptures, called the Tripitaka, or Three Baskets, or divisions of the teachings: the Life of Buddha, the Discipline, and the Teachings. It was probably not for many years that all the scriptures were reduced to writing.

A Second Council was held in Vaisali about
a hundred years later to settle various questions
of discipline, at which Council serious differences
in belief began to emerge and from that time the
division into sects has been characteristic.

The teachings concerning the Order had been
so simple and explicit that apparently it continued without much change for many centuries;
in fact the rules are much the same today as then.
At first they had no fixed home but during most
of the year wandered about teaching and begging
their food, coming together only during the
rainy season, in the refuges given to the Order
by their wealthy friends. These shelters gradually became monasteries with centralized administration, ceremonial and membership. But
even down to the present, all monks are welcome
to shelter and food at any monastery, under conditions of course. Although in later centuries
the Order became divided into scores of sects
with very divergent interpretation of the scriptures, monks would still be welcome at each
other's monasteries and would live together in
amity. The monks were to live a strictly celibate
life, have no extra clothing or property of any
kind, and use the gradually accumulating property of the Order for the common use and welfare. They were not to accept gifts of money
individually or occupy places of honor or author-

ity. They were not to preach before formal audiences, but were encouraged to teach by conversation and by sermons to the brethren and at casual gatherings.

Thus the Order continued for two centuries gaining believers steadily throughout northern India, and individual monks wandered far beyond these limits to southern India, the Panjab, and Kashmir.

Gautama died in 483 B. C. India at that time was the seat of one of the four great civilizations of antiquity. These four were China, India, Assyria and Persia, and the Egypt-Grecian civilization of the Mediterranean. These populous and learned and wealthy people were united by great trade routes. Every new exploration and discovery and deciphering of inscriptions reveals and confirms the fact that they were in comparatively free intercommunication. A most remarkable fact of this particular time, the Sixth and Fifth Centuries B. C. was the widespread emergence of great intellectual leaders. In China there were Laotzu and Confucius; in India, the writers of the Upanishads and Gautama; in Greece, Pythagoras, Socrates and Plato; in Palestine, the great prophets; in Egypt there was the Thrice Great Master Hermes. Whether the pollen of the thoughts of one culture was carried on the winds along the great trade routes to cross fertilize and stimulate another can never be proven, perhaps, historically, but most certainly the scholarship of one nation was carried far afield by wandering scholars and monks and prisoners of war and merchants. Not to have so happened would have been the greater marvel.

India at the time of Gautama's death was distracted by innumerable tribal wars such as practically destroyed the Shakyas and Kosalas. At that time there was apparently no great centralized authority in all India. No doubt the rumors of the gathering of great armies by Xerxes and Cyrus for the invasion of Greece must have penetrated thus far. Certainly the rumble of the great conquests of Alexander as his legions steadily advanced over Persia and into the Panjab, coming to a halt at her very doors, must have sent a shock of wonder and fear to her extreme confines.

Everywhere that Alexander went he not only conquered, he ruled wisely and forcefully, giving due participation to native princes. He introduced European enterprise, improved roads, cleared navigation, revived commerce and planted Greek learning and culture everywhere. This is significant for our purpose for it opened the way for all future time for the free exchange of learning. He took particular interest in exploring new systems of thought and accumulating scientific facts and art treasures. But if Greek culture spread eastward as far as the Indus river in India, it is also true that Indian learning and philosophies penetrated as far westward as Greece and Egypt.

At the death of Alexander his conquests were divided among his generals, Asia falling to the lot of Saleucus. For twenty years there were devastating wars in Greece and Egypt and Asia Minor, but in the Euphrates valley there was fairly stable government. Saleucus made his capitol at Antioch on the Orontes, on the great trade route from India to Egypt, and for many centuries it was one of the most populous and rich cities of the world. The rule of the Saleucidae in parts of western Asia was with power and success for a thousand years thereafter.

A certain low-caste adventurer, Chandragupta, said by some to have been the son of a barber and by others to have been the son of a king by a low-caste woman, in some way made his way into the camp of Alexander while he was still in the Panjab, with a plan for the conquest of the whole of India; but as the Macedonians were tired of their long absence from Greece, his plan was not accepted and he was driven from the camp. For some years he wandered among the tribes of northern India, a soldier of fortune. Slowly he gained authority over the northern tribes and was able to conquer the Panjab from the Grecian rulers. Then he extended his conquests to the Ganges river and finally conquered the whole of northern India. Both he and his son ruled wisely and powerfully; they were not mere military adventurers but proved to be men of vision and idealism. Finally the Empire fell to the grandson, Asoka (264-227 B. C.), who proved to be one of the world's great rulers. He extended the limits of his empire to include all of India and some of Kashmir and Afghanistan. At first he was a man of war but became disgusted with its bloodshed and disorder and, having received from his father a liking for Buddhism, embraced it, first as a layman and later as a full monk, and honored his profession by the sincerity of his life. He applied his faith in the Eightfold Path to works of wisdom and mercy: the digging of wells, the opening of roads, planting of shade trees and medicinal herbs, the encouragement of learning, especially of medicine and the art of healing; finally he became an enthusiastic missionary of the Buddhist faith. He sent out and supported envoys and missionaries to all his provinces and then to neighboring kingdoms of Ceylon, where he sent his daughter and son-in-law, to Kashmir and Tibet on the north, to Persia, Antioch and Egypt and Greece on the west. He built elaborate and beautiful monuments at all the notable places of the Buddha's earthly life, and erected stone pillars at many strategic points of his empire. On these stone pillars were engraved the faith and purpose of his life and they remain to this day incontrovertible proof of the doctrine and life of the Buddha.

One of his notable acts was to call a Third Council of the Order. He evidently called it to consider the evil of division into so many sects and other gross departures from the primitive simplicity of the Master's teachings. From the stone inscriptions we know that Asoka was a believer in these simple teachings and the result of the Council was to establish as canonical the assured Pali scriptures. The Council took steps for the increased reduction to writing and wider circulation of these teachings. But later history shows all too clearly that the over-ruled minority were not subdued, for from that time developed a clear distinction between the primitive teachings as preserved in Ceylon and Burma and which is known as Hinayana, and the more involved and metaphysical form that is maintained in Tibet, Mongolia, China, Korea and Japan.

From these stone inscriptions we learn that Asoka had sent his embassies and missionaries not only to the Yonas (the emigrant Greek population), but also to far away Asia Minor,

Egypt and Greece. One of these inscriptions as translated by Smith reads:

No. 5. (His missionaries) are engaged among people of all sects in promoting the establishment of piety, the progress of piety, and the welfare and happiness of the lieges, as well the Yonas, Kambojas, Gandharas, Rashtrikas, Pitanikas, and other nations on my borders.

No. 13. Even upon the forest tribes in his dominions, His Majesty has compassion and he seeks their conversion, inasmuch as the might even of His Majesty is based on conversion. . . . . (It has been communicated) even to where the Greek king named Antiocus dwells (Antioch), and beyond that Antiocus to where dwell the four kings severally named Ptolemy, Antigonus, Magas and Alexander; and in the south to the kings of etc. . . . . Even in these regions where the envoys of His Majesty do not penetrate there are men who now practice and will continue to practice the Law of Piety. . . .

From this time on Buddhist ideas became frequent in many forms of European literature and culture. Its traces are seen particularly in Pythagorianism, Stoicism, in the Hermetic and Kabalistic literature of Egypt and in the Therapeutae of Alexandria.

It is seen also and unmistakably in the celibate community of the Essenes in the Jordan valley along the great trade route from India and Persia to Egypt. It is to be remembered also that Judea was a Persian Province for several hundred years at just this time. Concerning this sect of the Essenes we will now turn our attention.

CHAPTER SEVEN

THE SEMI-BUDDHIST ESSENES

In our last chapter we saw that about the latter half of the Third Century B. C. a great Indian Emperor Asoka had become a Buddhist monk and was sending letters, envoys and missionary embassies to the Greek kings at Antioch and Egypt recommending to their attention the true religion of the Buddha. We saw, also, that in Egypt there were various Gnostic and secret cults like the followers of the Thrice Great Master Hermes, the Pythagoraeans and the Therapeutae, all of whom were indoctrinated with Indian and Persian philosophical, metaphysical and cult ideas. Among these secret brotherhoods were the Essenes of the Jordan valley, who have particular interest to us because of their relation to the Hebrew worship of Jehovah and because of their influence in the lives of John the Baptist and Jesus, and hence in the origin of Christianity.

Their beginning is lost in the dim past; many of the ancient records speak of this, some ascribing their origin to Moses himself. There are scores of suggestions as to the origin of the name. Scholars trace it through root words:

to be silent, to be mysterious, endowed with the gift of prophecy, a physician, a member of the fraternity.   Then there are some scholars who find the derivation from some form of the Hebrew word, 'hadishim,' meaning pure or holy. Among these are the historians Philo and Josephus.   The latter refers to them as 'the third sect, *who really seem to practice holiness,* are called Essenes.'

The best scholars of today are inclined to find the origin of the name in the old name of the more devout believers in the Law, who were known as the Chassidim.   Later on, in early Maccabaean times, they are referred to as the Asidaeans.   At that time they are represented to be a brotherhood who are very zealous for the full practice of the Law.   They were not so much politically patriotic as they were religiously loyal. This name does not appear after Maccabaean times, but in 166 B. C., in the days of Jonathan the Maccabee, a similar brotherhood are referred to as the Essenes.   This makes the name to have been derived from words meaning, 'the associates,' 'those who have disciplined the body,' 'the pure ones.'

At about the same time the word Pharisee also appeared.   Some scholars believe that the name Pharisee is derived from the Persian Parsi, and that they were so named because they were the

portion of the priesthood and devout believers
in the Law who had been influenced by Parsi
teachings during the 200 years that Judea had
been a Persian Province; the Sadducees being
the section who remained loyal to the ancient
Hebrew tradition. It is significant that the
names of angels were treasured by both Parsi
and Pharisees and were ignored by the Sadducees. In this connection it is interesting to note
that some of the things that separate the Pharisees from the Essenes are the same that separate
the Buddhists from the Parsi. The Pharisees
were the scholars and the rank and file of the
priesthood who accepted ' the traditions of the
elders' as well as the Law, and who were the
support of the temple worship. On the whole
they were sincere and devout, quite different
from the impression one gets from the estimate
in the Gospels. The Sadducees were the conservative wing who gradually came to monopolize
the High-Priestly office and its enormous revenues. While they were conservative as regards
the Law, because of their wealth and power and
tendency to adopt Greek culture, they were
sticklers rather for the letter of the Law than
for its spirit. With the destruction of the temple
and break up of the Jews as a nation, the Sadducees disappeared. The Pharisees being the
scholars survived as rabbis and were the basis

of the whole rabbinic system. The Essenes survived until 40 A. D. when they disappeared, being absorbed, no doubt, among the followers of John the Baptiser and the rising brotherhoods of Christians.

The Persian conquest would explain the separation of the Pharisees and Sadducees, but something else must have happened to explain the separation of Pharisees and Essenes; that something was the great wave of Indian thought that rolled over Egypt, Syria and Greece with the return of the Babylonian captivity and the tremendous increase of intercommunication that followed Alexander's conquest of Asia. It is a historical fact that after all the efforts of the Persians to recolonize the Jews in Palestine the best part remained at and near Babylon. From that time on there was the vast movement of the Jews of the Dispersion going and coming with the merchandise of the world and bringing tribute to the temple feasts.

Then as we have seen there was the effort of King Asoka to send Buddhist missionaries and envoys to the kings at Antioch and Egypt. In spite of the almost fanatical zeal of the Jews for proselyting, there were carried far more Indian ideas to Europe and to Egypt than Grecian and Egyptian and Jewish ideas to Persia and India. These fertilizing and fecundating influences

were at their height in the Third and Second
Centuries B.C. and registered themselves in the
rise of new sects and philosophies everywhere.
In Egypt they appeared as the Hermetic and
Kabalistic and Pythagoraean schools of thought;
in Greece and Rome by the extraordinary rise
of the mystery-religions, the worship of Isis and
Osiris, of Dionysius and the Eleusis, of the Great
Mother and Mithra; it showed itself in the
transformation of Greek philosophy of pre-
Aristotle type to later Stoicism, Neo-Pytha-
goraeanism and Neo-Platonism, all of which
were a blend of Oriental mysticism and Greek
thought and which never again could be sep-
arated.

Among all this ' chemicalization ' of ideas none
is more difficult to follow than the reactions of
Persian dualism, with its contrasted ideas of
light and darkness, good and evil, wisdom and
ignorance; and Hindu speculations as to the
nature of the soul; and Buddhist ideas with its
emphasis on the things of this world, purity of
ethical life, fate, and laws of kindness; with
Jewish ideas of monotheism, ceremonial purity
and the moral commands of the Law. That these
Persian and Indian ideas did register on Jewish
thought is undeniable, in spite of the denials and
ignoring of European scholarship with all its
Christian intolerance and exclusively Mediter-

ranean culture. A good place to look for it is in this semi-Buddhistic brotherhood of Essenes, to which Christianity must also look for its origin.

The original sources for information concerning the Essenes are principally three: Philo, Pliny and Josephus. Pliny's reference is very brief and unimportant. As the others are quite independent and each contain essential facts, the whole of each is given. The translations are taken from an essay by Dr. Ginsberg published in 1864.

Philo was an Alexandrian Jew who lived somewhere between the years 20 B. C. and 40 A. D. He was a very learned scholar, the head of a school devoted to the reconciliation of Hebrew theism and Greek philosophy. His teachings were undoubtedly known to Paul and the writer of John's Gospel. As he never visited Palestine his knowledge of the Essenes is from hearsay. There are two accounts purporting to be by Philo, one of which was in a treatise entitled, Apology for the Jews, which is lost except as quoted by Eusebius, and as the part quoted has nothing to do with the real Palestine Essenes it is omitted. The other account is in a treatise entitled, 'Every Virtuous Man Is Free.' It is as follows.

Palestine, and Syria too, which are inhabited by no
slight portion of the numerous population of the Jews, are
not barren of virtue. There are some among them called
Essenes—in number more than 4000—from, as I think, an
incorrect derivation from the Greek hononym 'hosiotes,'
holiness, because they are above all others worshippers of
God. They do not sacrifice any animals, but rather endeavor to make their own minds fit for holy offering.
They, in the first place, live in villages, avoiding cities
on account of the habitual wickedness of the citizens,
being sensible that as disease is contracted from breathing
an impure atmosphere, so an incurable impression is made
on the soul in such evil company. Some of them cultivate
the earth, others are engaged in those diverse arts which
promote peace, thus benefiting themselves and their neigh-
bors. They do not lay up treasures of gold or silver, nor
do they acquire large portions of land out of a desire for
revenues, but provide themselves only with the absolute
necessaries of life. Although they are almost the only
persons of all mankind who are without wealth and possessions—and this by their own choice rather than want
of success—yet they regard themselves as the richest,
because they hold that the supply of our wants and contentment of mind, are riches, as in truth they are.

No maker of arrows, darts, spears, swords, helmets,
breastplates, or shields—no manufacturer of arms or
engines of war, nor any man whatever who makes things
belonging to war, or even such things as might lead to
wickedness in times of peace, is to be found among them.
Traffic, inn-keeping, or navigation, they never so much as
dream of, because they repudiate every inducement to
covetousness. There is not a single slave to be found
among them, for all are free and mutually serve each
other. They condemn owners of slaves, not only as in-
just, inasmuch as they corrupt the principle of equality, but
also as impius, because they destroy the law of nature,
which like a mother brought forth and nourished all alike,
and made them all legitimate brethren, not only in word
but in deed; but this relationship, treacherous covetousness,
rendered overbearing by success, has destroyed by en-

gendering enmity instead of cordiality, and hatred instead of love.

They leave the logical part of philosophy, as in no respect necessary for the acquisition of virtue, to the word catchers; and the natural part, as being too difficult for human nature, to the astrological babblers, excepting that part of it which treats upon the existence of God and the origin of the universe; but the ethical part they thoroughly work out themselves, using as their guides the laws which their fathers inherited, and which it would have been impossible for the human mind to have devised without divine inspiration. Herein they instruct themselves at all times, but more especially on the seventh day. For the seventh day is held holy, on which they abstain from all other work, and go to the sacred places called synagogues, sit according to order, the younger below the elder, and listen with becoming attention. Then one takes the Bible and reads it, and another of those who have the most experience comes forward and expounds it, passing over that which is not generally known, for they philosophise on most things in symbols according to ancient zeal.

They are instructed in piety, holiness, righteousness, economy, politics, in knowledge of what is truly good, bad and indifferent, to choose things that are necessary, and to avoid the contrary. They use therein a threefold rule and definition, viz: love of God, love of virtue, love of mankind. Of their love to God, they give innumerable demonstrations—*e. g.* their constant and unalterable holiness throughout the whole of their life; their avoidance of oaths and falsehoods, and their firm belief that God is the source of all good, but of nothing evil. Of their love of virtue they give proofs in their contempt for money, fame, and pleasures, their continence, endurance, in their satisfying their wants easily, simplicity, cheerfulness of temper, modesty, firmness, order, and everything of the kind. As instances of their love to man, are to be mentioned their benevolence, equality, and their having all things in common, which is beyond all description, and about which it will not be out of place to speak here a little.

First, then, no one has his own house, so that it belongs
to all. For, besides that, they all live together in sodali-
ties; it is also open to the brotherhood who come from
other places. Moreover, they have all one common treasury and store of provisions, common garments, and common
food for all who eat together. Such a mode of sleeping
together, living together, and eating together, could not
be so easily established in fact among any other people;
and indeed it would be impossible. For whatever they receive daily, if they work for wares, they do not retain it as
their own, but give it to the common stock, and let every
one that likes make common use of it. Those that are sick
are not neglected because they can earn nothing, but have
what is necessary for their aid from the common stock,
so that they ever fare richly without wanting anything.
They manifest respect, reverence and care for the aged,
just as children do for their parents, administrating to
them a thousand times with all plentifulness both with
their hands and their counsels in their old age.

Such champions of virtue does a philosophy produce
which is free from the sublety of Greek word-splitting,
and which deals with subjects tending to the exercise of
praiseworthy actions, and giving rise to invincible freedom. This was seen in the fact that many tyrants have
risen from time to time in that country, differing in character and conduct. Some of them endeavoured to surpass
in ferocity wild beasts; they omitted no manner of barbar-
ity, they sacrificed the vanquished in whole troops, or,
like butchers, cut off pieces and limbs of those who were
still living, and did not leave off till retributive justice,
which governs the affairs of men, plunged them into similar miseries. Others, again, converted their frenzy and
madness into a different kind of wickedness. They
adopted an inexpressible bitterness, spake gently, and
betrayed a ferocious temper under the mask of gentle
language; they fawned like poisonous dogs and brought
about irremediable miseries, leaving behind them in the
cities, as monuments of their impiety and hatred of mankind, the never to be forgotten miseries. But neither the
cruel tyrant nor the wily hypocrite could get any advan-

tage over the said brotherhood of Essenes, or holy ones, but disarmed by the virtues of these men, all recognized them as independent and free by nature, praised their common meals and community of goods, which surpasses all description, and is an evident proof of a perfect and a very happy life.

The next source is Flavius Josephus, the well known Jewish historian; born in Jerusalem about 37 A. D. For a time he was connected with the Essenes for the purpose of study, although he was never admitted to a knowledge of their secret books and ritual. Allowance must be made for his well known habit of saying things and interpreting them in a way to win favor with the Greeks whom he greatly admired. His references are scattered in numerous books. The first selection is taken from his ' Jewish Wars,' book ii, chapter viii, sec. 2-13.

There are three sects of philosophers among the Jews. The followers of the first are called Pharisees, of the second Sadducees, and of the third, who really seem to practice holiness, Essenes. Jews by birth, they love each other more than the others. They reject pleasure as an evil, and regard continence and not yielding to passions as virtues. They despise marriage, and adopt the children of others while still tender and susceptible of instruction, and regard them as their own relations, and train them in their practices. They do not, however, repudiate marriage, and its consequent succession of the race in themselves; but they are afraid of the lasciviousness of women, and are persuaded that none of them preserve their fidelity to one man.

Sec. 3. They despise riches, have all things in common in a very admirable manner, and there is not one to be found among them who is richer than another; for it is a law that those who enter the sect must give up their possessions to the society as common property, so that there is not to be seen among them all, either the abjectness of poverty or the distinction of riches; but as every man's goods are cast into a common treasury, they all, like brothers, have one patrimony. They regard ointment as defiling; and if one happens to be annointed against his will, he immediately wipes it off his body. To be unadorned but dressed in white they regard as commendable. They have stewards of their common property, appointed by general election, and everyone without distinction is proposed for all the offices.

Sec. 4. They have no separate city, but some of them live anywhere; and if any of the society come from other places, whatever they have lies open for them, just as if it were their own; and they go to those they have never seen before as if they had been most intimate. Hence they take nothing with them when they go on a journey, but arms for defence against robbers.(?) A steward is appointed in every city to provide strangers with clothes and other necessaries. The keeping and appearance of their body are such as of children brought up in fear; they change neither garments nor shoes till they are worn out or made unfit by time. They neither sell nor buy anything among themselves, but every one gives of that which he has to him that wants, and gets from him that which he needs; and even without requital they can freely take whatever they want.

Sec. 5. Their piety toward God is extraordinary, for they never speak about worldly matters before the sun rises, but offer up with their faces toward it, some of the prayers transmitted by their forefathers, as if they supplicated it to rise. Hereupon, they are all sent by the overseers, everyone in the department in which he is skilled; and, having diligently labored until the fifth hour, assemble together in one place, girt round with their linen apron, and have a baptism with cold water. After this lustration they resort to a special house, in which no one of another house is admitted, and go to the refectory purified as to a holy temple. Having quietly taken their seats, the baker gives every one a loaf of bread according to order, and the cook places before each one a dish with one sort of food. The priest commences with prayer, and no one is allowed to taste his food before grace is said. He also returns thanks after the meal; for both at the commencement and at the conclusion they praise God as the giver of their food. Whereupon they put off their white garments as if they were sacred, and betake themselves again to their work till evening. On returning again they take their supper together, at which strangers, who happen to be in the place, are allowed to sit down with them. No noise or tumult ever desecrates their house, but they let everyone take part in the conversation in turn; and the silence of those within appears to those who are without as some awful mystery. The cause of this is the uninterrupted sobriety, as well as the fact that their eating and drinking are so measured out as just to suffice the cravings of nature.

Sec. 6. Whilst they do nothing without the injunctions of their overseers, yet there are two things in which they have free action, viz., helping the needy, and showing mercy; to help the deserving when they are in want, and to give food to the hungry, they have perfect liberty; but to give anything to their relations they are not allowed without permission of the overseers. They are just dispensers of their anger, curbers of their passions, representatives of fidelity, ministers of peace; and every word with them is of more force than an oath. They avoid taking an oath, and regard it as worse than perjury; for they say that he who is not to be believed without calling on God for witness is already condemned of falsehood. They take extraordinarily great pains in studying the writings of the ancients, and select that which is especially beneficial to both soul and body; hence they investigate medical roots and the property of minerals for the cure of distempers.

Sec. 7. When anyone desires to enter the sect, he is not immediately admitted, but although he has to remain a whole year without, yet he is obliged to observe their

ascetic rules of living, and they give him an axe (hoe?),
an apron as mentioned above, and a white garment. If
he has given proof of continance during this time, he ap-
proaches nearer to their life and partakes of the holier
water of purification; but is still not yet admitted to their
common table. Having thus given proof of his persever-
ance, his conduct is tested two more years, and, if found
worthy, he is admitted into the society. But before he
touches the common meal, he swears, by most awful oaths,
first to fear God, and next to exercise justice toward all
men—neither to wrong any one of his own accord nor by
the command of others; always to detest the wicked and
side with the righteous; ever to keep faith inviolable with
all men, especially with those in authority, for no one
comes to office without the will of God; not to be proud of
his power not to outshine his subordinates, either in his
garments or in greater finery, if he himself should attain
to office; always to love truth and strive to reclaim all
liars; to keep his hand clear from stealing, and his mind
from unholy gain; not to conceal anything from the brotherhood, nor disclose anything belonging to them to those
without, though it were at the hazard of his life. He
has, moreover, to swear not to communicate to any one
their doctrines in any other way than he has received
them; to abstain from robbing the commonwealth; and
equally to preserve the writings of the society and the
names of the angels. By such oaths they bind those who
enter the brotherhood.

Sec. 8. Such as are caught in heinous sins are excommunicated from the society; and the excommunicated frequently die a miserable death. For, being bound by oaths
and customs, they cannot receive food from any out of the
society, so that they are forced to eat herbs, till their
bodies being famished with hunger, they perish. Hence
they compassionately receive many of them again when
they are at their last gasp, thinking that suffering, approaching death, is sufficient for their sins.

Sec. 9. In their verdicts they are most exact and just,
and never give sentence if there are less than a hundred
of the brotherhood present: but what is then decreed is

then irrevocable. Next to God they have the highest
veneration for the law-giver, Moses, and punish with death
anyone who blasphemes him. To submit to the elders
and to a majority they regard as a duty: hence, when ten
of them sit together, no one will speak if the other nine
do not agree to it. They avoid spitting before the face,
or to the right hand, and are also stricter than all other
Jews not to touch any labor on the Sabbath day—for
they not only prepare their Sabbath-day's food the day
before, that they may not kindle a fire on that day, but
they will not move a vessel out of its place nor go to ease
nature. On all other days they dig a pit of a foot deep
with the spade (such an one being given to the novice),
and having covered it all round with a cover, that it may
not offend the divine rays, they set themselves over it, and
then put the earth that was dug out, again into the pit;
and do this, after having chosen the most lonely places.
And although the voiding of bodily excrements is natural,
yet it is their custom to bathe after it, as if they had been
defiled.

Sec. 10. They are divided, according to the time of
leading this mode of life, into four different classes, and
the juniors are so much inferior to the seniors, that the
latter must wash themselves when they happen to touch
the former, as if they had been defiled by a stranger. They
live to a great age, so that many of them live to be a
hundred years—arising from the simplicity of their diet,
as it appears to me, and from their order. They despise
suffering, and overcome pain by fortitude. Death, if connected with honor, they look upon as better than long life.
Of the firmness of their minds in all cases the war with
the Romans has given ample proof; in which, though they
were tortured, racked, burned, squeezed, and subject to all
the instruments of torment that they might be forced to
blaspheme the name of the law-giver or eat what was for-
bidden, yet they could not be made to do either of them;
nor would they even once flatter their tormentors or shed
a tear, but, smiling through their torments and mocking
their tormentors, they cheerfully yielded up their souls
as those who would soon receive them back again.

Sec. 11. For they firmly believe that the bodies perish and their substance is not enduring, but that the souls are immortal—continue for ever and come out of the most subtle ether—are enveloped by their bodies, to which they are attracted through natural inclination, as if by hedges— and that when freed from the bonds of the body, they, as if released from a long servitude, rejoice and mount upwards. In harmony with the opinion of the Greeks, they say that for the good souls there is a life beyond the ocean, and a region which is never molested either with showers or snow or intense heat—is always refreshed with the gentle gales of wind constantly breathing from the ocean; whilst to the wicked souls they assign a dark and cold corner, full of never ceasing punishments. And it seems to be according to the same opinion that the Greeks assign to their valiant men, whom they called heroes and demi-gods, the Island of the Blessed, but to the souls of the wicked the regions of the impius in Hades; as also their fables speak of several there punished, as Sysiphus and Tantalus and Ixion and Tityus. This they teach, partly because they believe that the souls are immortal, and partly for the encouragement of virtue and the discouragement of vice. For good men are made better in their lives by the hope of reward after death, whilst the passions of the wicked are restrained by the fear they are in that, although they should be concealed in this life, after death they must suffer everlasting punishment. This is the doctrine of the Essenes about the soul—possessing thereby an irresistible bait for those who have once tasted their philosophy.

Sec. 12. There are also some among them who undertake to foretell future events, having been brought up from their youth in the study of the Sacred Scriptures, in divers purifications, and in the sayings of the prophets; and it is very seldom that they fail in their predictions.

Sec. 13. There is also another order of Essenes who, in their way of living, customs, and laws exactly agrees with the others, excepting only that they differ from them about marriage. For they believe that they who do not marry cut off the principal part of human life—that is, succession—especially that, if all were of the same opinion, the whole race would soon be extinguished. They, however, try their spouses for three years, and after giving evidence, by three natural purgations, that they are fit to bear children, they marry them. They have no connubial intercourse with them with child, to show that they do not marry to gratify lust, but only to have children. The women, too, have their garments on when they have baths, just as the men have on their aprons. Such are the customs of this brotherhood.

From 'Antiquities,' book xiii, chapter v, section 9.

At this time (166 B.C.) there were three sects among the Jews, differing in their opinion about human affairs. The first was called the sect of the Pharisees, the second the sect of the Sadducees, the third the sect of the Essenes. The Pharisees affirm that some things only, but not all, are the work of fate, and some are in our own power, whether they should take place or whether they should not occur; the sect of the Essenes maintains that fate governs all things, and that nothing can befall man contrary to its determination and will; while the Sadducees reject fate, saying that there is no such thing, and that human events do not proceed from it, and ascribe all to ourselves, so that ourselves are the cause of our fortunes, and receive what is evil from our own inconsiderateness.

From 'Antiquities,' book xviii, chapter i, section 5.

The doctrine of the Essenes delights in leaving all to God. They regard the soul as immortal, and say that the attainment of virtue must be fought for with all the might. Although they send consecrated gifts to the temple, yet they never bring any sacrifice on account of the different rules of purity which they observe; hence, being excluded from the common sanctuary, they offer sacrifices in themselves (spiritually). Otherwise, they are in their manner of life the best of men, and employ themselves wholly in the labor of agriculture. Their uprightness is to be admired above all others who endeavor to practice virtue; such uprightness, which is by no means to be found among the Greeks and foreigners, is not of recent date, but has existed among them from times of yore, striving most serupulously not to disturb the community of goods, and that the rich should not enjoy more of the common property than the poor. This is the conduct of this people who are more than four thousand in number. They never marry wives, nor endeavor after the possession of property; For they believe that the latter leads to injustice, and the former yields opportunities for domestic discord. Living by themselves they serve each other. They choose good men, who are also priests, to be the stewards of their incomes and the produce of the fields, as well as to procure the corn and food. They do not differ at all in their living, but are more like those whom the Dacae call Polistae.

There are other short references to the Essenes in the works of Josephus, but as they add little to our knowledge of their customs and ideas, they are omitted. Besides these sources there are many scraps in the Mishna, the Talmud, the Midrashim and other Hebrew writings. From these we gather that the Essenes were in good and regular standing as true worshippers of Jehovah and careful observers of the Law. This is confirmed by the high estimation in which they were held by Pharisees and Sadducees alike.

The following are outstanding instances of their conformity to the national cult:

1. Highest regard for the Law, using the Scriptures for worship, comment and study.

2. Scrupulous observance of the Sabbath.

3. Their chief aim to be fit temples for the Divine Spirit.

4. Formal avowal at initiation of love for God and reverence for Moses.

5. Looking forward for the coming of Elias and the Messiah.

6. References in their early morning hymn to the Creator and Lord.

7. Punctilious observance of the Levitical code of purity, by frequent washings and bathing.

8. Practices concerning purity when relieving the bowels and burying the excrement; use of apron when doing so and when bathing.

9. Habits as to spitting.

10. Special regard for the gift of prophecy.

There are also outstanding differences, almost all of which have resemblances to Buddhist practices, as for instance:

1. Preservation of a middle path between excessive asceticism and free indulgence.

2. Aim to attain through self control of desire to the highest possible moral and ethical purity.

3. Living outside cities in brotherhoods.

4. Practice of the celibate life, in recognition of the advantage it offered as a spiritual discipline; but they honored marriage for procreation

and arranged for certain believers to live in the married state.

5. Giving up all private possessions, and as a brotherhood avoiding unnecessary accumulation of property.

6. No distinctions of rich and poor, master and servant.

7. Strict community of property.

8. Reprobation of slavery and war.

9. No recourse to violence or use of arms even in self defence.

10. Refusal to engage in any unethical labor.

11. Food limited to the simplest vegetables, fruit and bread, of which they partook sparingly at two meals only.

12. Refusal to eat meat or drink wine of any kind.

13. Clothing limited to the simplest and used until worn out.

14. Use of cosmetics and annointing oils prohibited.

15. Restriction of unnecessary conversation, avoidance of oaths and emphatic asservations.

16. Solemn oath at initiation to live up to the brotherhood's ideals of conduct.

17. Among these ideals of conduct are the following which closely resemble corresponding ideals among the Buddhists: To be earnest, determined to advance to the highest degree of self

control as expressed in a life of kindness, resignation to fate, love of virtue; contempt for fame or power or riches, or sensual pleasures; practice of temperance, modesty, humility, simplicity, contentment of mind, cheerfulness, benevolence and generosity toward brothers and strangers alike, love for all the brethren, tender regard for children and the sick and aged, tolerant, cherishing good-will toward all alike, serenity, equanimity, and firmness under insult or oppression; abhorrence of all deception and unchaste thoughts; and a cheerful looking forward to death as a release. They ascribe these rules as having come from the ' fathers.'

18. Discouragement of all speculative philosophy and peering into unknowable things as detrimental to a serene and devout life.

19. Employment of symbolism rather than dialectics in teaching.

20. Interpretation of life in terms of ethics and kindness than in moral and legalistic terms of good and evil.

21. They made use of education as it bears on the necessary things for attaining piety, purity, self-control, kindness, serenity and cheerfulness.

22. Interest in the study and practice of the art of healing.

23. They studied certain secret books about healing sickness, the mysteries of nature, hidden

wisdom, the celestial hierarchy and the practice of meditation.

24. They had no separate priesthood.

25. Their early morning hymn had at least three references to characteristically Buddhist teachings.

26. Repudiation of animal sacrifices.

27. The government of the brotherhood was entirely fraternal.

28. Misbehavior was considered by the full company; confession was encouraged and admonition given, only in extreme cases was expulsion enforced, and subject to return upon due repentance.

29. Recruits principally from gifts of boy children to the order, who were carefully brought up; also by voluntary applicants.

30. Probation of three years before initiation.

31. There are numerous references to similarity of beliefs; concerned especially with an ethical way of life but also hold in reserve various esoteric teachings; Conception of God is less anthropomorphic than the common Jewish conception, more universal and indefinable; God is the source of all good, never of evil; subject to law, never arbitrary.

32. Their conception of the body holds it to be impermanent, but to be preserved in purity and its desires to be strictly restrained; its pains

to be borne with fortitude and looked upon as a virtue.

33. The soul neither is immortal, nor is not immortal. This assertion needs to be amplified. Before the Third Century B. C. the Jews gave almost no thought to a personal life after death. In a general way they had a conception of other worlds and of national rewards and punishments, and of the coming again of Elias and of a Messiah, but gave almost no thought to the metaphysical implications of these general thoughts. It was the impact of the new ideas from the East that awakened their interest. There are indications that it was this very question that caused the division of the ancient Asidaeans into the Pharisees, Sadducees and Essenes. The Sadducees insisted on free will and denied any such thing as resurrection of either body or soul, i.e., they were sticklers for the old conservative ideas. The Pharisees, however, followed a middle path on both these questions. They apparently believed in a limited reincarnation of the souls of good men in other bodies, and in the resurrection of both body and soul in a life hereafter of eternal rewards for the good, and eternal punishment for the evil. It is not at all certain whether they believed in an actual resurrection of the body or not. They certainly looked for the reappearing of Elias before the coming of

the Messiah, but whether as the resurrection of the old body, or reincarnation in a new body is not clear. At the other extreme the Essenes were definitely believers in fate and in the end of the body, and in some form of reincarnation. What exactly they believed is buried with the other secrets they guarded so carefully. They deprecated all discussion of such questions except as it bore on the practical way of life. Their attitude toward death was one of cheerful anticipation as a release from the bonds of body and matter, and in the hope of ultimately attaining a state of bliss. This belief does not clash necessarily with the ideas of either Pharisees or Sadducees, and at the same time it may be vastly different from either, and in full accord with Buddhist ideas of Karma, rebirth and Nirvana. The metaphysical and philosophical implications of such questions being new to the Jews were doubtless not very well understood or fine distinctions valued. Certainly their characteristic cheerfulness and serenity in the face of death is more like the Buddhist than it is like the Jewish, or the Christian for that matter.

34. Belief in intermediary beings between the Supreme Deity and man, and below the world also, i.e., in angelic and demoniac worlds.

35. Belief that fate governs all things and that nothing happens to man but by its determination.

36. Conception of a higher realm to which they may attain.

37. Conception that virtue and the reward of virtue must be fought for with all the might.

38. Claim that their secret teachings were received from the forefathers; this has no meaning if it refers to Moses.

39. Recognition of an ancient tradition that was radically different from the official and national Law of Moses.

40. Death considered as an advantage to be looked forward to with serene anticipation.

41. Essenes, like Buddhists, held in highest respect by all grades of people.

In conclusion to this extended chapter on the Essenes it may be said that the object is not to prove that the Essenes were Buddhists, but only that while they are the descendants of the more devoted and spiritually minded of the ancient Hebrews, differing little from the Pharisees in religion, they had been very considerably influenced from unknown Buddhist sources. Because there is no direct historic evidence we have been obliged to show it by the extended reference to circumstantial evidence. It is exceedingly significant that in the list of resemblances to Judaism and to Buddhism, the resemblances to Buddhism outnumber the former three to one. Note especially that the historians to whom we are indebted for information were ignorant apparently of any such thing as Buddhism and saw the Essenes only through Greek and Jewish eyes. Moreover of the Christian writers who have touched upon (or ignored) the subject, those who know anything about Buddhism are almost unanimous in seeing decided resemblances, and those who have an exclusive Mediterranean culture are the ones who either ignore it, or pass it by as improbable. But recent research by the philologist, Reitzenstein, strongly confirms the fact that there were stronger influences, than had hitherto been supposed, of oriental ideas at work among the early Jewish sects, especially among the followers of John the Baptist. The orientalist, Lidzbarski, who has edited and translated the writings of the gnostic sect of Mandaeans, points out that they originated in the Jordan valley and are nothing other than the sect of John the Baptiser. The Mandaeans also called themselves Nasoreans, which means ' observers.' This is the very title that is given to Jesus three or four times in the New Testament and indicates that Jesus was, in the beginning, known to be a follower of the Essenes.

It is in this semi-Buddhist community of the Essenes, then, that the founders of Christianity, John the Baptist and Jesus, were brought up.

No other hypothesis compares with this when we seek the source of those peculiar and characteristic marks of pre-Pauline Christianity. Certainly Christianity drew more from the Essenes than from any other Jewish sect, and it is not strange that with the rise of the followers of John as a sect, and of the Christians as an offshoot sect, that the Essenes as an independent sect, disappeared. Some students seem inclined to think that the oriental influence was more gnostic and Babylonian than Buddhist, which it was in the later days; but only Buddhism accounts for the early dominant characteristic of economic and ethical practices of loving self-control, kindness, and communism. If Christians should be proud of anything, they should be proud of their Essene origin.

CHAPTER EIGHT

JUDEA AT THE TIME OF JESUS.

No ADEQUATE idea of the beginnings of Christianity can be obtained without taking into consideration the social and political disorders of the times. Palestine is only a small country but it lies across the land route between three continents; the merchants and armies of Greece and Rome, of Assyria and Persia and India, must pass over it to reach Egypt. Hence from the earliest times it has been the location of wars and turmoil. We must pass over the earlier days which were no less tumultuous than the later ones, and come to the return from the Babylonian exile under Ezra and Nehemiah, the latter part of the Sixth Century B. C. Even with the backing of Persia the returned exiles had to build with one hand and fight with the other. After that came the invasion of Alexander, the wars of Antiochus, the rise and conquests of the Maccabaean princes to be the kings and high-priests of a united and independent nation, but at the cost of untold bloodshed and suffering.

This was followed by the Roman conquest and the establishment of their authority by the Herodian line of kings. The Herods were Jews, but from Edom, and were of those who forsook both their religion and culture to be the followers of Roman emperors and Greek culture. Besides the invading Romans of those centuries and immediately following, the armies of the Arabian kings and Parthian emperors also ravaged the country. With the success at last of the Herodian kings there was an end for the time being of invasion from without, but the Herods ruled with an extreme of ambitious, cruel and unjust fear and hatred. The Maccabaeans had ruled with a hand of iron and had slaughtered the pagan natives of the captured cities, but the wrath of the Herods slaughtered both friends and foes alike. At the destruction of the old temple in 63 B. C., it is said that 12,000 were killed, many burnt to death in the temple, and both men and women slain in the streets.

At the death of Herod the Great in 6 B. C., only two years before the birth of Jesus, there was a climax of horror. No one knows how many lives had been lost in those three or four centuries, doubtless they were numbered in the hundreds of thousands, and they included the choicest of her patriot sons. To provide the treasure required to build the great temple and palaces in Jerusalem (he had a mania for building monumental buildings in outside Greek cities as well), Herod not only taxed excessively, he confiscated private wealth wherever he could locate it and find excuse for doing so.

He assassinated the brother of his beloved Queen; he assassinated the husband of his own sister; he assassinated Hyrcanus II, the grandfather of his Queen, when Hyrcanus was eighty-two years of age; and later he butchered her own mother, a second husband of his sister, and these were but the highest in rank; no record could be kept of those whose lineage was unimportant, so awful was his fear and fury. It is true Herod built the magnificent temple at tremendous cost, not leveling a mountain to provide space for it, but by enormous buttressed walls making the mountain higher and wider for the temple's courts and colonnades. He did not do it for any love for the Jews or respect for the worship of Jehovah, but to enhance the glory of his capital. And then to undo any credit he might have had from the Jews for his generosity, he crowned the entrance with a golden image of the imperial Roman eagle. The Jews were furious and, in one of many efforts to remove it, forty were burnt alive, the deed being ordered when Herod was mortally sick. As he lay dying he ordered the death of his own son and the death of one each from all the great and noble families of Jerusalem.

Archelaus, his son, seized the throne, and while

waiting for Caesar's confirmation, angered at a
gathering of the populace in the temple, he
ordered his mercenary soldiers to disperse them.
Over three thousand were killed in the temple,
'and their blood was mingled with the blood of
the temple sacrifices.' This revealed the true
character of the son and intensified the hatred
of the Jews for the whole Herodian line. The
Jews sent a delegation of fifty of their wealthiest
nobles and merchants to Rome, where they were
joined by all the Jews resident there, of whom
there were over 8000, to protest against the confirmation of Archelaus, and to beg Caesar to
make Judea a part of the Roman province of
Syria, and so be governed by a Roman procurator.

Then followed a succession of uprisings and
awful suppressions by Roman armies. The worst
of these was the one on Pentecost when the
pilgrims joined with the populace to resist a most
unjust act of Sabrinus, the Roman general.
Using this as an excuse, he invaded the temple
courts, to preserve order he said, but the result
of it was the destruction of the magnificent
temple which had been finished only six years.
His soldiers looted the temple, Sabrinus taking
400 gold talents for his share, and in the confla-
gration that followed a thousand lost their lives
and other thousands were slaughtered in the

streets before the trouble ended. This was almost at the birth of Jesus.

All Judea was out of control, riots and bloodshed were incessant, to be crushed relentlessly by Roman resources. Little by little open acts were seen to be futile; people seemed cowed by the terrible severity of the Roman rule, but underneath the fire burned and secret bands of patriots, hiding in the caves and fastnesses of Galilee and the Jordan valley, would appear suddenly to strike terror to caravans and isolated bands of soldiers and unprotected palaces. To the Roman historians they were robbers and 'knife-carriers,' but in fact were as devoted patriots as the Maccabees themselves. Any descendant of the Maccabees could gather a following at any time, especially in Galilee where the nature of the country added to their safety. On the other hand the Roman officials in their effort to preserve order ruled most ruthlessly, slaughtering men, women and children, combatants and peaceful villagers alike.

For ten years Archelaus ruled as Ethnach, but not as king. He was like the father in his love for building great buildings, but was far more profligate and licentious. At last his conduct was so outrageous that the Emperor exiled him to Gaul and confiscated his wealth. But the Jews found to their dismay that the rule of a

Roman procurator was just as bad as a Herodian king. The taxes were made heavier and more general, and high-priestly robes were held by the Procurator to be released only at the three festivals. The Jews openly protested in riots that fell little short of rebellion. Gradually the bands consolidated into a new sect of patriots, called the Zealots, whose single object was revolt against Roman rule, any time, anywhere it was feasible. The leader was Judas the Galilæan. After two procurators had failed to establish order, Pontius Pilate was appointed (26-36 A. D.) and it was during his term that Jesus lived his brief public life of one short year, ended with his crucifixion. Pontius Pilate was vainglorious, insolent, given to unreasonable oppression and humiliations, robbery and ' incessant and unmitigated cruelty.' He carried the imperial insignia at the head of his troops into the precincts of the temple in the certainty that it would excite bloodshed, and it was only removed at Caesar's direct command. He appropriated the dedicated funds of the temple and when the people protested his soldiers killed them. His downfall came when he was more brutal than common in suppressing a religious gathering at Samaria. These riots and uprisings and wars went on until 44 A. D. when they took on a more serious character which came to a climax with the destruction of Jerusalem in 70 A. D. The Jews were slaughtered, sold into slavery, dispersed into captivity; and it marked the break up of the Jews as a nation; save only the futile uprising under Bar Kochbar a few years later, and then the end. For so small a country as Judea the loss of life was appalling, but it is to be remembered that the Jews who lived in Palestine were but a fraction of the Jews of the Dispersion, who were scattered from Spain to India and Rome to Alexandria.

But there is another side to the story that is less creditable to the Jews. They were ever a stubborn and obstinate people, and, as against the Romans and their tools the renegrade Herods, their stubbornness was unbelievable. Many of the causes of their riots seem unimportant to us of these more tolerant days. With the death of her noblest patriots, the dispersal of her sons with wider vision to far away gentile cities, the average of the Jews remaining in Palestine was of a weaker and more fanatic type, given to extremes of religious fanaticism and patriotic fury. Besides the terrors of war there had been the more demoralizing effect of a great earthquake in 30 B. C., and three years of extreme famine and pestilence. Oppression, fear, suffering, all combined to add to the ranks of excited, hysterical and turbulent religious devotees.

It is true the Romans failed utterly to understand the religious bigotry and obsession of the people for the sanctity of the least letter of the Law and the least stone of the temple. The Romans could never understand why the Jews should object so obstinately to such inconsequential things as the Imperial insignia, the Olympian games, the temples of other peoples, the theaters, but rave they did to the blind sacrifice of their very lives. It seemed to the Romans and to many others of more liberal days, to be a mark of innate obstinacy and rebellious nature. In every popular outbreak of religious fervor, Romans saw the preliminaries of a political revolt that must be crushed without mercy. So things went from bad to worse making of the people extremes of religious fanatics, visionary patriots, moralists and mystics, all waiting expectantly for the coming of a Messiah and 'the salvation of the Lord.'

Those who returned from the captivity brought back the prophecies of Jeremiah and the Second Isaiah: 'The riches of the Gentiles' were to come to Israel, 'all nations should bow down to them with faces to the ground,' 'enemies should be cut off and great should be the welfare of her children,' 'And great,' should be, 'the peace of Jerusalem.'

Instead of this the centuries had brought wars,

tumult, earthquakes, famine, pestilence, poverty, rivers of blood, humiliations, and slavery. Is it any wonder that these terrible times and terrible experiences should have served to increase the number of 'introverts' and insane, who sought escape from the suffering of external conditions by recourse to fantasies and obsessions. Out of the despair of such disappointment, the ancient ideas and hopes of the coming of a 'son of David,' who should lead them out of their humiliation into a restoration of the glories of David and Solomon, only increased. Even more, the successes of Alexander and the Caesars only served to widen their vision of the Messianic hope.

For a time the rise of the Maccabees had served to warrant these hopes, but with their fall, the conquest of Rome and the rule of the Herods, these hopes, in the minds of the more thoughtful at least, were seen to be hopeless. Gradually there grew up a more spiritual vision of the messianic hope, in the coming of a divine and eschatalogical Messiah. Instead of a political kingdom it was to be a Kingdom of Heaven, not for individuals but for Israel as a nation. A glorious future, a new age, the Good Times of the Messiah, must be the recompense for the disappointment and suffering.

Blurred in with this was another conception,

namely, the identification of the Kingdom of God
with 'the Age to come,' when, after the resurrection there was to be a final Judgment Day
with its rewards of eternal life of bliss and eternal
suffering, in which the Sovereignty of God
crowded out the idea of the earthly rule of a
Messiah.

The more ignorant peasantry clung to the old
prophetic idea of an earthly kingdom established
above the nations in worldly power and glory,
with a princely son of David at its head. But
to the more thoughtful Jews, who better appreciated the desperate straits to which they were
reduced, the new vision of a more spiritual kingdom had come. This is seen in many a volume
of apocalyptic and eschatalogic literature that
characterized the century before and the century
after the birth of Jesus. The Pharisees thought
of it in the light of the covenant relation of Israel
as a nation. This was John's idea also, only he
added and stressed the call to individual repentance and 'works meet for repentance,' as a
preliminary requisite.

At the birth of Jesus the nation was divided
into four rather distinct groups. There was a
relatively small group of wealthy and aristocratic families who controlled the high-priestly
office. They had embraced Greek culture and,
while clinging to the letter of the Law, had ad-

apted themselves to the time and kept as well as they could in favor with the Romans. These were the Sadducees, rich, worldly and proud.

The Pharisees included most of the priesthood and scribes and educated people generally. They were very religious and devoted to the temple ceremonials, but had yielded somewhat to the times by adding the 'traditions of the elders' and adopting a more lenient interpretation of the Law. From them in later days came the rabbis and the whole rabbinical system. But they, like the Sadducees, held the common people in contempt and placed more emphasis on ceremonial observance than on the ethical code.

The Zealots were the young, hot-headed patriots, cherishing hatred for Romans and Edomites and the rich and ruling classes alike. They were true followers of the Law even if ignorant of its more elaborate demands, only they added to their respect for the Law the solemn duty to defend it by the sword. To the Romans and Sadducees they were robbers and 'knife-carriers,' but in reality, up to their light and ability, they were the patriots of the day.

Finally there were the Essenes, small in numbers, and living serene and untroubled in the midst of the riots and bloodshed, in their brotherhoods among the mountain fastnesses of the Engedi. They avoided the cities and the temple with its bloody sacrifices, abhorred war and violence, had all things in common, and made it their first duty to be kind to the poor and sick. They believed in fate, in the impermanence of the body, but in some form of rebirth. The Zealots were trying to impose socialism by force, but the Essenes were living a kinder communism among themselves and had built up perhaps the first successful Utopia in the history of the world.

Both John the Baptist and Jesus were brought up among these Essenes and became members of the brotherhood. They learned the ways and the secret teachings of the Essenes which served to modify their inherited religious ideas and give an impetus to their particular missions.

CHAPTER NINE

INTRODUCTION TO THE LIFE OF JESUS

THE sources of information about Jesus are very few and untrustworthy. We get most information from the Gospels, but they are late and so overlaid with Christian propaganda that they are unreliable and deceiving.

There is a very early reference in Josephus but even this short reference has obvious signs of interpolations, which we take the liberty of omitting. He writes:

> Now there was about this time, Jesus, a wise man . . . . for he was a doer of wonderful works, a teacher of such men as receive the truth with pleasure. He drew over to him many of the Jews and many of the Gentiles . . . . When Pilate, at the suggestion of the principal men among us, had condemned him to the cross, those that loved him from the first never ceased . . . . and the sect of the Christians, so named from him, are not extinct even now.

The Talmud had scattered references to him, but as they were mostly concerned with stories about his illegitimate birth (even his noble qualities and deeds of kindness were often turned into subjects of mirth), it is evident that they were written after Christianity had become a matter of annoying concern. There are also a number of Midrashim and Baraitae that refer in more

detail to his illegitimate birth, but these appear
to date as late as 150 A. D.   The references by
Celus, the Roman historian, have the same hostile bias and are also of late date.

Perhaps the earliest authentic references are
in Paul's letters.   According to accepted chron-
ology, Paul lived at the same time as Jesus —
he became his disciple within three years of his
death — and was acquainted with Peter, and
with James, 'the Lord's cousin,' and other disciples, yet strange to say he says almost nothing
about Jesus' earthly life.   He was so engrossed
with his vision of the Risen Christ and its theistic
implications, that he ignored almost entirely the
historic life.   Perhaps it had for Paul only the
value of a suggestion, and perhaps John and
Jesus actually lived very much earlier than the
Gospels indicate.

The early Church Fathers, Justin Martyr and
Papias wrote about 135 A. D. but make very
few references and they carry almost no information.

The great source is the Gospels.   It is now
generally agreed that the original Mark must
have been written about the time of the destruction of Jerusalem, 70 A. D.   Next comes Matthew about 90 A. D., then Luke about 110 A. D.
Matthew and Luke both drew from Mark and
from another early account which is known as

'Q' and which is now lost except as it can be recovered from Matthew and Luke. But all of these Gospels are so evidently written to defend the Christian conception that Jesus was the Son of God and the fulfillment of Jewish prophecy, that they must be used for recovering the historic Jesus with the greatest caution. The Gospel of John was written much later, perhaps as late as 150 A. D. and was openly designed to make reasonable the author's mystical theism.

According to Mark and Q, which are the safest to go by, Jesus was born about 4 B. C. of a Galilean carpenter and his newly wed wife Mary. In neither of these two sources is anything said from which one could infer that there was anything unusual about the birth of Jesus. But the detailed legends in both Matthew and Luke which were written soon after, of miraculous happenings, especially the vision that came to Mary and her conception by the Holy Ghost, the fact of her being pregnant before her marriage, and the wide-spread belief among Jews that Jesus was of illegitimate birth, and the large place that the virgin birth plays in Christian theology, all throw doubt on the fullness and accuracy of Mark's account.

Because of the modern science of Psychoanalysis more attention is now being paid to the *psychic health* of Jesus and John, with the result that still more doubt is cast on the probability of Joseph being the father of Jesus. So much is made in the Gospels of Mary's conception by the Holy Spirit, of Jesus' self assertion of messiahship and divinity, and of his sinlessness; and there is so much in the formulation and development of Christianity, which all depend on the normalty of Jesus' mind, or ought to so depend, for any evidential value they may have, that the facts ought to be carefully sought out and considered.

Dr. Beatrice Hinkle in her book entitled, 'Recreating the Individual,' divides humans into two great classes, extroverts and introverts. Concerning the latter class she writes as follows:

The introverts' close association of feeling with the personal ego causes an intense awareness which, to the simple extrovert, is quite unknown; and this, together with the realization of his inadequacy and uncertainty toward the outside world, produces a peculiar sense of inferiority which, however deeply hidden, is a fundamental characteristic of the introverted personality. The overcoming of this and the painful effect which it produces is the chief aim of the psyche, the deep underlying purpose of all its strivings, and in this struggle lies the dominant motive of the life — 'the will-to-power.' This continuous striving Adler calls 'the masculine protest' and it very concretely describes the effect which so largely dominates the life of the introvert in either masculine or feminine form. For it is not actual power in the real world that he seeks — that is the extrovert's desire — but the overcoming of the unbearable feeling of inferiority which appears to him to depend upon the domination of the object.

Again, Dr. Hinkle writes:

The thought function of the introvert is used as the primary means of adaptation, for without the thought function he could not adapt at all. It concerns itself with the welfare of the ego, and that which affects its position in the world. Secondarily, it creates ideas and concepts of its own, having no relation to facts; it postulates abstractions and ideal conditions, and obeys wholly other laws than those belonging to the external reality.

Such an introvert may be characteristically either emotional or intellectual according as to which of these faculties predominates. In either case he will be moved primarily by intuition rather than by logic; he will arrive at definite conclusions more by seeing visions than by reasoned logic, and in expressing himself he will use symbols rather than logical premises. If the intellectual faculty is stronger than the emotional he will have visions of truth, of prophecy, of awareness, that will appear to the more practical extrovert, as flashes of genius. Such an one, also, if the sex libido is inhibited from following a natural course, will very likely sublimate its tremendous energy into some form of religious mysticism. Such an one will have an exaggerated ego-sense, which when associated with inferiors, the poor, the sick, or children, will be excessively kind and sympathetic, but with his equals or superiors will be irritable, self-conscious and, if thwarted or unjustly treated or even observing injustice toward others, will flash into sudden bursts of anger and loss of self control. Such an one may apparently be perfectly normal, a little inclined to be egoistic and brilliant at times and then again, discouraged, timid and retiring at others. They are often extremely clever at hiding their mental unsoundness by frequent retirement into solitude, running away from success as well as from failure. Such an one will easily pass over the line of sanity into religious fanaticism and paranoia. He may conceive himself to be some great personality, to be the voice or mind or instrument of some supreme revelation of truth; obsession easily passing over into hallucination. Particular attention is called to these psychologic facts, which if found in any particular personality subtract from the value of his ideas and teachings and authority: instead of carrying conviction they will to that extent carry doubt.

It does not follow, however, that an introvert is necessarily of lesser value than an extrovert; in fact the very opposite is often the case. The introvert is in fact a higher and later development in the biological series, because the extrovert's superiority lies in his better adaptability on the physical plane, while the introvert is better adapted on the psychic and spiritual planes. The extrovert becomes a world conqueror, but the introvert becomes a world savior.

CHAPTER TEN

LIVES OF JOHN THE BAPTIST AND JESUS

AT SOME unknown time in the reign of Herod the Great, it fell to the lot of a humble old priest named Zacharias to offer the incense at the temple service. As this honor came but once or twice in a lifetime, he was naturally excited and his mind was filled with awe and emotion. He entered the curtains of the Holy Place and ascended the steps of the altar; the worshippers waiting expectantly for the smoke to ascend and for the priest to reappear swinging the censer. They saw the smoke arise but no priest appeared. They waited with increasing impatience and at last Zacharias appeared, not with swinging censer, but as one dazed and speechless. There beside the brazen altar he had seen a vision and heard a voice saying that his prayer was answered. The excitement of the occasion and the vision and the voice had been too much for the old priest and he had fallen in an epileptic fit. When he came to himself, he found his speech organs paralyzed, and he emerged dazed and trembling and making signs with his hands.

Later his wife gave birth to a son that was christened John. In the joy and thanksgiving of the hour, just as suddenly as it had failed, Zacharias recovered the use of his voice. When this happened and of the early life of John we know nothing. It is written that he lived in the desert until he suddenly appeared in the Jordan valley, an eccentric preacher. He was clothed in sheepskin and ate only the vegetable food he could find in the wilderness. From his behavior, the emphasis he placed on baptism, purity of life and poverty, he had evidently been with the Essenes. This was the more probable because their principal brotherhoods were located not far from the head of the Dead Sea and near the supposed home of Zacharias. Their notable piety and purity of life, austerity of living and religious zeal would appeal to John's epileptic and priestly father and to his own psycopathic nature. The only thing against this supposition is the violent nature of his preaching, but that can be explained by his abnormality, for no sane man would address the crowds who gathered at his place of baptism: 'You brood of vipers, who told you to flee from the wrath to come?' Or what sane man would publicly denounce his sovereign, in those days of violence and injustice, for shameful acts of unchastity?

Crowds flocked to hear his rabid denunciation of sin, his insistent urge to repentance and purity of life, and his clarion call to make a clear way for the coming of the Messiah. He denied that he himself was the Lord; He was only a voice crying in the wilderness; after him would come a greater than he, who would baptize with fire and the Holy Spirit.

Very soon after the death of Herod another interesting birth took place. The Gospels link it in with the birth of John, but more and more scholars are inclined to separate the two by at least ten or fifteen years. Somewhere about 4 B. C. an elderly Galilean carpenter became betrothed to a maiden by the name of Mary. There is no doubt that she cherished the hope common among Jewish maidens, that she might be the mother of the long expected Messiah. It is not surprising that in the excitement of the times incident to the change of rulers from Herod the Great to Archelaus, and the stir caused by the preaching of John the Baptist, and the emotional strain of her own betrothal, that she should have a vision of bearing a son who should be the Messiah. The Gospels speak of her making a visit to the home of her aunt, who was Elizabeth, the mother of John, just before her marriage and that when she returned the affianced husband noticed her condition and hesitated to marry her, but was miraculously encouraged to do so. How much of this is true and how much mythical it is hard to say. The child when it came was

called, Jesus. From the beginning Jesus was a
precocious child given to doing odd and unusual
things, and uttering strange and unexpected
ideas. The only thing recorded of his childhood
in the Gospels, was that when he was taken to
the temple when he was twelve or thirteen years
old and the family was returning, they missed
him from the company. They searched for him
a day or two before he was found, and when at
last he was found he was in the temple in a group
of elderly men, answering and asking questions
of such an unusual nature that they were aston-
ished and filled with curiosity. When his mother
questioned him as to why he had left their party,
his reply was baffling and somewhat impertinent.
The record continues, ' Then he went down along
with them to Nazareth and did as he was told,'
as though that was a little unusual. Then the
record says, ' His mother hid everything in her
heart,' as though perplexed and in anxious fore-
boding she wondered what would come of his odd
behavior. While nothing more is said of his
youth in the Gospels, there are scores of reputed
acts and sayings handed down in the uncanonical
writings of the years that followed, and all hinted
at some unusual and precocious abnormality.

When Jesus was about thirty years of age, he
appeared one day in the crowd about John on
the banks of the Jordan, and asked to be bap-

tized. The question at once arises, where had he been during the thirteen to fifteen years of his youth and early manhood. No one knows. The record speaks of other children in the family of Joseph, five boys and at least two girls, but whether any of them, or all, were children of an earlier marriage is not stated. The record makes no further reference to Joseph. At Capernaum Jesus is referred to as ' a carpenter and the son of a carpenter,' and Justin Martyr writes that there were some of the ox yokes and goads that he had made still in existence in his day. But other facts would indicate that he was looked upon as a stranger in Nazareth. His appearance in the synagog excited curiosity and he is evidently a stranger to his mother's home. He never after goes there or has anything to do with either his mother or his half-brothers. They come at one time to restrain him and to take him away by force, but Jesus disowns them and will have nothing to do with them. At his crucifixion, it is mentioned that his mother was present among the other women and that Jesus asks John to care for her, but as the reference is only in John's Gospel it is doubtful.

On the contrary there are many indications that he had spent a long time with the Essenes. When he appears it is as a strange roving figure, living a celibate life, going off frequently by himself. He has the Essene habit of doing deeds of kindness and preaching by the wayside, and he has an amazing gift for healing. Later he sends his disciples out two by two for preaching, with no extra clothing or shoes or money, and with instructions to ask for hospitality when they need it, which is precisely the Essene rule. Like the Essenes he feels free to accept hospitality from any one that offers it, from the rich, the publicans, sinners; and talks with prostitutes and beggars and the sick with no fear of personal defilement. And like the Essenes he often retires to solitude.

Another indication of association with the Essenes is seen in his relations with John. When Jesus appears at the Jordan, John recognizes him, and by his words reveals the fact that he is acquainted with thoughts in Jesus' mind that Jesus generally tries to keep concealed, namely, his obsession that he is the Messiah. This would indicate that John and Jesus had been associated with each other and had shared with each other their inmost thoughts and visions. .

Both John and Jesus were profonndly moved by the inherited faith of their ancestors and by the common type of hope of the approaching end of the age. John goes forth ' to prepare the way of the Lord,' and later Jesus follows.

As Jesus comes out of the water from his baptism he has a vision that brings to a focus all the brooding thoughts and aspirations of his young manhood. He sees a dove circling over him and alighting on him and a voice saying, ' This is my beloved son; this day have I begotten thee.' All students see in this incident a turning point in the life of Jesus. Before, doubtless, he had had brooding thoughts prompted by the ' inferiority complex ' of his introvert nature, using as symbol the common idea of the long expected Messiah. Suddenly under the influence of the excitement of the occasion and the mass psychology of the observing crowd, the vision flashed on his excited mind: *he* was actually the Messiah! It was a case of an extraordinary mind supplying from fantasy the solution of his mental distress and bringing balm to his wounded vanity.

Jesus immediately, true to type, avoids asserting his newly recognized dignity, and returns to the wilderness to brood over it. For forty days he struggles with the doubts and fears and urgings of an upset and disordered mind. The main questions and decisions slowly take form, and in every case (again typical of the introvert), the decisions take the form of a physical evasion, finding the solution in the realm of spirit. If he accepts the task, how will he be fed? The temptation is to test his power, see if he can turn stones into bread. Then he recalls his childhood teachings of Jehovah's care of the people of Israel in the wilderness, that man did not live by bread alone, and the decision comes, to trust his Heavenly Father's care.

The second worry was as to his ability to act the part of a Messiah. He was keenly conscious of his inferiority as a fighting patriot like the Galilaean Zealots; what could he do? He was tempted to throw in his lot with the Zealots and fight a desperate fight the world's way through blood and hate and suffering, to final victory — an imperial crown and rule like unto David and Solomon of old. Opposing this is the recollection of the quiet days among the Essene brothers. Their ideas of loving goodwill and self-controlled submission to fate, be it what it will, flooded his soul with healing balm; he would trust the unfolding of the Divine will.

The third problem was as to his personal safety. He was well acquainted with the recent interpretations of the ancient prophecies of the coming of the Messiah: there was to be an end of the Age, to be preceded by suffering and untold miseries, to be followed by the appearance of the Lord supported by legions of angels and coming in clouds of glory. But would he be physically able to endure the preliminary suffering? Just as he recognized his inferiority as the leader of a forlorn hope in desperate battle, so he recognized his weakness when brought face to face with physical pain. The temptation was to make a test of some kind, to see if, as it was written, 'the angels would bear him up, lest he dash his foot against a stone.' His decision was still to trust his Heavenly Father.

From this time Jesus began to wander about the country, talking with those he met and doing strange deeds of healing. His casual conversations and preaching were very much like John's, probably he had no other idea at first than to further John's proclamation; he certainly did no baptizing himself, or anything else that looked like setting up a rival movement. He became known as Jesus, the Nasoraean, that is, an observer of the baptism and rules of the Essenes. There is nothing in the Gospels to tell how long this continued; it might have been a year or two before John's imprisonment and death. After that time the preaching of Jesus was very much more aggressive and egoistic, and, as a consequence, in a few months culminated with his own arrest and crucifixion.

According to the Gospels, at first his mind was not at all clear whether to publicly announce his messiahship, or not to do so. On the whole his introvert nature led him to conceal it, but gradually differences between John's preaching and his began to emerge. The call to repentance was decreasingly emphasized, and where John always referred to the near coming of the Kingdom, Jesus always referred to it as already present, if they had eyes to see. This is the new conception that Jesus added to the current understanding of the Kingdom of Heaven, and to the end he struggled with parables to awaken an interest in it and a desire for it.

Perhaps in his Essene days he had heard of Gautama's habit of referring to himself as the Tathagata, ' he-who-has thus attained,' and so he always referred to himself as ' the son of man.' The Hebrew words simply meant, ' this man,' and Jesus often used them in the sense of ' I,' or ' me.' At other times he used them as the name of the Messiah; and still other times he used them as referring to the appearance of the Messiah after the end of the Age. But in every instance there is a concealed reference to himself — of this there is no doubt.

He expected, apparently, because of his ' works ' alone, that people would soon come to see that he must be the Messiah, and that following this recognition, there would be divine attestations of it, and the inauguration of the Good Times of the Messiah.

This was the state of his mind until the return of the disciples from their mission, when the fact was forced on him that he was to be disappointed

in the expectation of any immediate acceptance
of his messiahship. This state of mind was followed by the new conception, that the Good
Times of the Messiah was only to be ushered in
by his own death.

CHAPTER ELEVEN

THE LIFE OF JESUS, (Continued)

AFTER the temptation in the wilderness, Jesus lingered about for a time and then returned to his native village where, apparently, he was not very well known. He mingled with the villagers, speaking strange words and doing unexpected deeds of kindness. At a wedding where they were too poor to provide wine, Jesus secretly provided it and then tried to cover up his act.

He attended the synagog service on the Sabbath and, when they asked him to take part, he read the prophecy of the coming of the Messiah from Isaiah, and then interpreted it. At first the hearers were charmed by the grace of his words, but as he became more incoherent and began to denounce some of their favorite beliefs, and, in a veiled way, to associate himself with the Messiah, they became very angry and drove him from the village. He wandered about Galilee healing many sick and, speaking with authority, he ordered evil spirits to come out of the insane. He certainly had some unusual psychic power over sickness and between that and his words of sympathy for the poor and sick, great crowds began to gather about him. But as

often as he could he would go off alone. Some
of those he healed, in their gratitude, acclaimed
him to be Divine, or the Messiah, but he invari-
ably checked them. By this time some of his
boyhood relatives and friends left their work and
followed him and later on others did the same
until there were twelve who were with him more
or less of the time. Among them were a few
fishermen. Many of the legends that gathered
about him are concerned with the sea of Galilee;
he never went far away from it in the short year
of his public life.

Very soon his fame spread to more distant
places, and Pharisees and Scribes from Jerusalem came to investigate. One day when he
was in a house, the crowd became so great that
they had to open the roof to get a paralytic into
his presence. Instead of saying, 'be healed,' as
he usually did, he said, 'My son, your sins are
forgiven.' This aroused the ire of the Pharisees
and a dispute followed, but Jesus always seemed
able to silence his questioners.

It became increasingly noticeable that when
Jesus was alone with the villagers and the sick
he was kind and gentle, but when he was beset
by these Pharisees and Scribes with their trick
questions, he became excited and difficult to follow. He became more and more careless of the
strict letter of the ceremonial law and defended

his freedom with spirit and cleverness; often he seemed to take a delight in flouting their prejudices, as when he healed a man's withered hand on the Sabbath day. His eccentric behavior, and lack of respect for those of higher social rank, and the ease with which he could be led into radical opinions, soon led to the beginnings of opposition, and from that time those in authority sought means of getting rid of him.

Jesus withdrew with his disciples into the more remote parts of Galilee, but still the crowds followed him, often coming from distant places to be healed. The fame of his wonderful works and wise words and, at times, his strange and excited behavior, spread everywhere. Even his family sought him out and tried to restrain him by force, thinking that he was insane, but he would have nothing to do with them. The Scribes even charged him with being in league with the devil; them he denounced in anger, as serpents and vipers. This was one side of his strange character.

The other side was gentle and wise and considerate. God was to him no longer Jehovah, the Lord God Almighty, but was a Heavenly Father, and all men were brothers. It was the duty of all people to love God with all the heart and mind and strength, and to love the neighbor as the self. He talked of an overworld of love that he pictured in parables as the Kingdom of Heaven. It was like seed sown in a field that grows by night and in secret; it was like a mustard seed that grows to be a great tree; it was a treasure hid in a field to be searched for; it was within a man's own heart. When his disciples asked him why he taught in parables he explained that the truth could only be understood and accepted by those who were ready for it. This was an Essene doctrine, a part of their belief in cause and effect, a richer life following because of previous self-control, enlightenment coming as one was ready to receive it.

One evening in order to escape the crowds they went in a boat to the other side of the lake, and as Jesus was weary he fell asleep. A great wind suddenly sprang up and the boat was in danger; they woke Jesus and, just as suddenly as it had risen, the storm died away. Jesus petulantly scolded them for their lack of faith and they were afraid of him. There is nothing very remarkable about this, but it came to be thought of as a miracle and proof of his messianic claims. Then there were more astonishing healings and greater crowds followed him.

About this time John had been imprisoned by Herod, partly because of his intemperate denunciation of the King's morals, and partly because of the potential danger Herod saw in al-

lowing so influential a man to be free to stir up
trouble among the people. While he was shut
up in prison John had sent two of his disciples
to ask Jesus if he still felt certain that he was
the Messiah; Jesus replied rather evasively, but
calls attention to his acts and words and urges
John not to lose faith in him. Jesus takes advantage of the occasion to praise John very
highly and to assert that he is the reincarnation
of Elias, sent to prepare for the coming of the
Messiah.

Soon after, Herod beheaded John and when
Jesus heard of it, he seemed to see in it the
signal for a more energetic proclamation of his
own message. Jesus calls his disciples together
and after giving them instructions in exactly the
same terms used by the Essenes, he bestows
power on them to heal the sick, and sends them
forth to spread the call for repentance and to
proclaim the nearness of the Kingdom.

After a time the disciples returned to Jesus
jubilant with the success they had had in the
ministry of healing but saying little as to the failure of the people to respond to the call to repentance. This omission had a profound effect on
Jesus. He had looked for a great response and
the beginnings of persecution, the sufferings
foretold by the prophets, that would precede the
coming of the Messiah. He called his disciples

apart to rest, but the crowds followed. His disciples seeing that the people were hungry urged
Jesus to send them away, but Jesus told the
disciples to feed them. They only had a few
loaves and a few small fish, but they did as Jesus
bade them, seated the people in groups, broke
the food in very small pieces and passed it among
them. Meanwhile Jesus had blessed the bread
and then talked to them one of his wonderful
talks about 'the bread of life that comes from
heaven.' In their interest they forgot their
hunger and went away satisfied.

Jesus sent his disciples across the lake to Bethsaida, while he went off by himself. But the
crowds found him out. The Pharisees tried to
entrap him with questions, but he was able to
silence them. His replies were often obscure and
baffling and he seemed to take delight in placing
the Pharisees in a bad light and irritating them.
In the evening his disciples would ask him to explain his replies, and he often scolded them for
their lack of understanding.

In his solitary wanderings, Jesus seldom went
very far away from his disciples; once he went to
the north to the land of Tyre and Sidon, and
tried to hide his identity, but he was recognized.
A woman asked him to heal her daughter and
he replied in a churlish manner, but when she
replied tactfully, he cured the girl. Then in the

same erratic manner he returned to Galilee and
on the way healed a deaf man by placing his
fingers in the man's ears and spitting on the
man's tongue. When he rejoined the disciples
they had no food; Jesus rebuked them for their
lack of faith, and spoke to them in an incoherent
manner about the leaven of the Pharisees. When
they failed to understand he charged them with
stupidity and after a time they ceased to talk
with him.

They crossed over to Bethsaida again and on
the way he treated a blind man by taking him
outside the village and spitting on his eyes and
asking him if he could see, and told the man not
to return to his native village. Then they went
across country to Caesara Philippi where he
suddenly asked his disciples, ' Who do people say
that I am?' They told him, ' Some say John
the Baptist, others say Elijah, or one of the
prophets.' Then he asked, ' Who do you think
I am?' Peter answered impulsively, ' Thou art
the Messiah.'

Jesus warned them not to speak of it publicly. Then he recalled to them that it was written that before the ' Son of Man ' could be revealed he must suffer great persecution and be
rejected by the elders and High-priest. As he
talked he became excited. Peter tried to restrain
him, but the others warned Peter not to say

anything more. It was too late, Jesus flashed
into anger and cried out, ' Get behind me, you
devil.'   At another time Jesus turned to the
crowd and harangued them about how people
must suffer with him, if they were to be his followers, and share in his glory when the Son of
Man should come in the glory of the Father with
the holy angels. ' I tell you,' he said, ' there are
some of you standing here who will not die before
they have seen the Kingdom come with power.'

A week later Jesus took Peter and John and
climbed a mountain. When they were resting on
the top, Jesus went into a kind of trance and
began talking to Moses and Elijah. The disciples were alarmed and Peter in an effort to
pacify him, suggested that they build shelters
and stay there for a time. Then a cloud settled
down on the mountain and they could hear Jesus
still talking to himself, repeating the words that
he had heard at his baptism, ' This is my son, the
Beloved; listen to him.'

As they returned down the mountain, Jesus
warned them not to say anything about what had
happened until the Son of Man should appear.
At the foot of the mountain there was a great
crowd awaiting him and he cured a boy troubled
with epilepsy. As soon as he was able to get
away from the crowd he again talked in an obscure manner about his coming rejection and its

following glory. They failed to understand what he was talking about, but were afraid to ask any questions. They had noted that ever since their return from their mission, Jesus had been more excitable, talked more about himself and had frequent spells of emotional extremes. He decided to return to the familiar scenes of his childhood. On the road his disciples were discussing among themselves as to who would be greatest in the Kingdom when the end did come. Jesus noticed it and in the evening had one of his good talks with them about humility, and unselfishness and helpful kindness. He warned them of the trials that awaited him, in which they too would suffer, and urged them to love one another.

In the days that followed, Jesus wandered about the familiar scenes of his childhood. He referred less and less to his early call to repentance, or to any expectation that the people would respond. The thought of his coming death depressed him, and his mind dwelt more and more on the wonders of the Kingdom that his death was to usher in. This state of mind, at times, made him more tender and kind toward the poor and the sick and little children, and his words then were of extreme beauty and sympathy.

Then, in contrast, there were frequent times when the Scribes and Pharisees heckled him, that he would rise to sudden bursts of anger. At one such time he bitterly denounced some of the villages where he had been, which had not responded in the way that he thought they ought to have responded. At such times he was easily led into arguments and the expression of radical opinions, such as his confused and contradictory words about divorce, and the need of forsaking wife and family and property, if they were to be his disciples. In Jesus' disordered mind the fact of the Kingdom was very real and vivid and the disciples, although not fully understanding, fell in with it. Peter reminded him once that they had left all to follow him, and asked what their reward was to be; and James and John asked for places of honor when he should come in glory, but Jesus reminded them of the persecution and pain that they must first suffer. He said,

You know that the rulers of the gentiles lord it over them, and their great ones exercise authority over them. Not so shall it be among you; but whosoever would be great among you shall be your minister, and whosoever would be first among you shall be your servant: even as the Son of Man came not to be ministered unto but to minister, and to give his life a ransom for many.

As the time for the great feast at Jerusalem drew near, the people began to ask his disciples if Jesus intended to go, and his step-brothers dared him to go. His disciples asked Jesus and he replied that he did not intend to go, but urged them to go. The opposition of the Pharisees had become so marked that the disciples did not think it safe to go, but Jesus encouraged them and they started. In a day or two Jesus changed his mind and followed after. When they asked for an explanation he replied enigmatically, that it was not proper for a prophet to die outside of Jerusalem. In the back of his mind, no doubt, was the Fifty-third Chapter of Isaiah: 'Jehovah hath laid on him the iniquity of us all, . . . because he poured out his soul unto death, and was numbered with the transgressors.' He became excited to such a degree that the disciples were in dismay, and even the crowd became frightened. A considerable company followed but not as many as formerly. The sick still sought him out and crowds followed him in curiosity to see what he would do next. The Pharisees redoubled their efforts to entrap him in words, and he talked more than ever about the Kingdom of Heaven and always in parables.

At Bethpage he sent two of his disciples to a nearby village to get an ass'es colt, and when they brought it, he mounted and rode in mimic state toward Jerusalem. The crowd, curious to see what would happen, spread their garments in the way and tore branches from the trees to wave in mock ceremony, shouting the old cry, 'Hosanna. Blessed be he who comes in the name of the Lord.'

In this mock state he rode to the temple and entered. Seeing the merchandise and the money-changing he became furious and seizing a small whip he upset the tables and drove out the money changers. He cried, 'Is it not written, my house shall be called a house of prayer? You have made of it a den of thieves.'

This naturally angered the temple authorities and they tried to arrest him, but the crowd sided with Jesus, and the temple servants became afraid. Jesus wandered about the temple, healing the sick, speaking parables about the Kingdom, disputing with the Pharisees, evidently expecting something to happen. But as nothing did, he left the temple and went to Bethany where he had friends, to spend the night. The next day he returned to the temple and the people thronged him in curious expectancy. Some of the temple officials asked him by what authority he acted as he did. In reply he questioned them and then refused to answer. He seemed to say things deliberately intended to anger them, but the authorities hesitated to arrest him for fear of exciting a riot and bringing the anger of the Romans upon them. The day passed in discussions and disputes, in the course of which he called the Scribes and Pharisees 'hypocrites' and 'offspring of vipers,' mingled with the utterance of wild and obscure proph-

ecies concerning impending sufferings and persecutions and destruction of the temple and the
city, and of his own death and exaltation.

Then there were moments of calm lucidity
when he spoke words of kindness and wisdom.
It was then that he told the parable of the sheep
and the goats, which runs as follows:

> . . . . Then shall the King say unto them on his right
> hand, come, ye blessed of my Father, inherit the kingdom
> prepared for you from the foundation of the world; for I
> was hungry and ye gave me to eat, I was thirsty and ye
> gave me drink, I was a stranger and ye took me in, naked
> and ye clothed me, I was sick and ye visited me, I was in
> prison and ye came unto me. Then shall the righteous say
> unto me, Lord, when saw we thee hungry and fed thee, or
> athirst and gave thee drink? . . . . And the King shall
> answer and say unto them, Verily, I say unto you, inas-
> much as ye did it unto one of my brethren, even unto the
> least, ye did it unto me.

At the close of the day Jesus left the temple
excited, weary and disappointed. As they came
to the crown of the hill, with the magnificent city
across the valley, they rested by the roadside.
Jesus was evidently perplexed and discouraged
at the failure of his expectations. The disciples
referred to some of the things he had said in the
temple, about its destruction, and asked when it
would take place. Jesus replied by warning
them soberly of the impending sufferings that
must first come before the end. 'Of the hour or
the day no one knows,' he said, 'Watch, in case

he comes suddenly and finds you asleep. Watch; I say it to you and I say it to all, watch.'

The next day they remained in Bethany, and in the evening he went with his disciples to a house in the city where the passover was to be eaten. As they sat at the table, Jesus was noticeably concerned and depressed. He seemed to have come to an awareness of the futility of his mission. He spoke earnestly to them of his coming death and uttered an impressive prayer. He blessed the food and in pathetic sorrow of heart gave them to eat. Then they went back to the Mount of Olives and in the silence of the night he turned aside into a secluded garden to pray. Jesus went apart from the others and in agony of spirit, prayed that he might be spared the coming suffering and end of his dreams. When he returned he found his companions sleeping, so he returned for another season of prayer. At last he awoke them and together they went out to the highway, where they found a mob of temple servants armed with sticks and clubs, sent to arrest him. Jesus quietly went with them to the palace of the High-priest, and late as it was, they proceeded to try and to condemn him. As they had little valid evidence of crime, the High-priest asked him directly if he claimed to be the Messiah. Jesus replied with the same air of authority he always carried, ' Yes,

I am; and what is more you will see the Son of
Man sitting at the right hand of power and coming in the clouds of heaven.'

As soon as morning came they took Jesus to
Pilate, the Roman Governor, and prayed that
he might confirm the sentence of death. Pilate
asked Jesus some questions but failed to find
anything worthy of death, and therefore sought
to release him, but the mob who had accompanied
the guard, protested and clamored for his death.
So Pilate did as they wished and turned Jesus
over to the Roman soldiers to be executed. Hearing that he was a man who set himself up to be
some sort of a king, and who was probably
crazy, they rigged up a throne, threw a purple
cloak about him, made a mimic crown of thorns,
and bowed down to him in cruel derision.

They led him to Golgotha and there they crucified the Son of Man. After a few hours only,
Jesus went into a comatose state and remained
as one in death.

Joseph of Arimathea, a councillor of wealth
and high rank, who was a devout Jew and some
think a lay member of the Essenes, went to
Pilate and asked for the body. Pilate was sur-
prised that Jesus should be so soon dead, for the
usual time of suffering is a full day, or even more,
so he sent to the captain of the guard to find out
if Jesus was really dead. The captain returned

word that he had been dead for some time, so the body was given to Joseph. The latter carried it to a new tomb, and with it sheets and linen to enwrap it. Evidently, but what follows is very uncertain, when Joseph and his servants reached the tomb they found life in the body. Perhaps they suspected it all the time, and knowing Pilate's private opinion of Jesus, had ventured, by a bribe, probably, to 'square it' with the guard and with Pilate, and thus to save Jesus even from the edge of the grave. After dark Jesus was secretly carried away.

After the Sabbath was over, when the women went to the tomb to embalm the body, they found it empty and the linen unused. A young man clothed in white, the usual dress of the Essene brothers, was in the garden and he told them that Jesus was risen from the dead and for his disciples to meet him in Galilee. Then he quietly slipped away.

Jesus was carried to some safe Essene retreat in Galilee where he recovered and afterward appeared to Peter and later to others of his disciples. This was only for a few days — the Jerusalem appearances are very doubtful — and then Jesus disappeared entirely. Perhaps he never fully recovered from the shock of the crucifixion; perhaps he returned to his old place among the Essenes and the quiet companionship of his flocks, perplexed, and baffled and disillusioned, there to die soon after unnoticed. It was the end of a strange and unbalanced life.

It is significant that among the early followers of both John the Baptist and Jesus — after their deaths — were many Essenes. Some scholars think that most of the early followers were Essenes.

There is no doubt but what Jesus was honest in thinking that he was the Messiah and that his death would usher in the coming of the Kingdom of Heaven and his exaltation, but, nevertheless, it was an illusion of an unbalanced mind. Nevertheless his life and death were not in vain nor futile; from their seed sprang a great world religion and with it the hope and comfort of innumerable men and women and children of many diverse races and times. His spirit of self-sacrificing love and submission to fate is still the hope of the world.

CHAPTER TWELVE

THE TEACHINGS OF JESUS.

JESUS was not a teacher in the sense that Gautama was, yet some of his ideas issued from an unusually clear faculty of spiritual intuition and unite to provide an attractive and convincing picture of Truth.

Let us recall that in the days of Jesus, Judea was filled by awful scenes of social, political and religious turmoil incident to the insane reaction of resistance and hate to Roman rule. In the background was a fanatical faith that they were the chosen people of Jehovah and that, in due time, the Messiah would come and save them out of their distresses and lead them to world power over their enemies and into great rejoicing. This had two effects upon the people. Some it aroused to fanatical fury as militant patriots; and in others, seeing the futility of resistance, it awakened feverish inner hopes and expectations that a Messiah would appear who would miraculously judge the nations and usher in a new age under the direct sovereignty of God. This was enough in itself to cause and did cause wide spread religious mania.

Let us recall, also, that Jesus had a personal

history of extreme religious devotion and seeing of visions. He was an illegitimate child, born of a mother who was a seer of visions, and was a second wife of a man much older than herself who already had a large family. Jesus grew up in an atmosphere of extremely unhappy conditions; his childhood, no doubt, was embittered by the taunts of older half-brothers because of his unfortunate birth. From the beginning we find him an odd, precocious child, and later revealing alternate states of elation and despondency, sense of inferiority and exaggerated egoism, shrinking from external problems of failure and success, into a solitude of prayer and day-dreams and fantasy.

To make the matter worse his mother had cherished the idea that her child, in a particular sense, was to be the savior of the world; instead she realized that he was odd and abnormal. Is it any wonder that at times, weary with the care of a large family of step-children, she became, toward Jesus, cross and unappreciative? In his after life, Jesus had little to do with her, and never refers to mother-love. This accounts for Jesus' tendency to make the father-image the symbol of his will-to-power. Was it because Joseph was kinder to him as a child? Was it Joseph, or the old priest Zacharias, who suggested that the boy be given to the Essenes to be brought up? It is certain that Jesus lived at some time among the Essenes, and it was the retired, quiet life among these kindly brothers that doubtless saved him from insanity. Among the Essenes, as among the Buddhists, when a boy entered the Order, he was adopted by some elder monk who looks after him and teaches him until old age when the boy in his turn cares for the monk. Perhaps this adopting father was a shepherd, and recognizing how ill fitted Jesus was for the usual work of the Essenes, had taught him to be a shepherd. Perhaps it was from him that Jesus got his fondness for the father symbol.

In this quiet, gentle, methodical, self-controlled and isolated life, his early childish repressions and unhappy experiences were forgotten and sank below the threshold of his conscious mind. But modern psychology has proven conclusively that these agonizing childish experiences are not ended by being forgotten. Rather are they damned up to be revealed years after in some morbid ill health, or erratic and perverse behavior. In the case of Jesus they appeared along with that side of his divided mind that was obsessed with the idea that he was the Messiah. So long as he lived among the Essene brothers, waking early, taking the cold baths of the purification rites, attending the devotional services and hymn to the rising sun, eating the simple

morning meal in silence, and then to the labor
of the day amid the solitude of the hill pastures
and the soothing company of the sheep, so long
were the forgotten experiences harmless. There
he came in contact with the peculiar teachings of
the brothers; which were tinged (the writer be-
lieves) by the wise and kindly ideas of the far
distant Buddha, which had percolated in to
sweeten and to harmonize their inherited ideas
of Jehovah, the tribal god of the Jews. There
he came in contact with new ideas of cause and
effect as an universal and predestinating principle; there he learned of rebirth and of a higher
life free from earth's pain and dissatisfaction and
unhappiness that was ever present and open to
all who would control their desires.

There he thought out, or more truly received
in through his marvelous intuitive faculties, the
revelation of Love's supremacy. In its warmth
the capricious tribal god of the Jews took on the
aspect of a Heavenly Father. His justice and
holiness changed to mercy and compassion, his
power and authority changed to loving good-
will and forgiveness. The old Mosaic Law lost
its negative severity in a new spirit of positive
co-operation: " It is written, ' thou shalt not kill,'
but I say unto you, love your enemies, do good
to those who despitefully use you and persecute
you." Under its magic, lust lost its power and

hate changed to willingness to lay down one's life for an enemy. In the light of Love the Messianic Kingdom, to whose coming all Jews looked forward as the end of the Roman servitude, became an ever present Realm of Love, something within, not something external, that unfolded in blessed freedom and joy as the soul yielded its selfish desires to Love's control. In its ozone the soul lost its clinging to selfness and comforts and even to life itself, to rest in the harmony and beauty of the Whole.

But with the awakening of John to become the fore-runner of the Messiah, perhaps with John's suggestion that he do the same, the disturbing thoughts began to emerge and to demand attention. The libido, not finding outlet through the normal sex channels, found an outlet in relieving his sense of inferiority by an illusion of greatness, that he, in a special sense, was ' the Son-of-Man.' By this outlet the sub-conscious and morbid ideas and compulsions found opportunity for escape and expression.

The early ideas of Jesus about the sovereignty of God and the coming of a Messiah were at first precisely the same as the current ideas among the more devout Jews. This common idea of the coming of the Messiah always included some terrible climax of suffering and judgment. As this involved too much brutal contact with

external conditions, his introvert nature shrank
from it and found refuge in day-dreams suggested by Essene teachings, of a different kind
of a God and a different kind of a Kingdom.
His God would be a Heavenly Father, his Kingdom would be a Kingdom of Love. Cherishing
this fantasy he naturally comforted his sense of
inferiority by illusions of greatness: God was
his Father, he was God's Son; it was his mission
to proclaim this new conception, and with its
proclamation the people would turn in repentance to a life of righteousness and joyful welcome for him as the Messiah. There would be
a preliminary time of persecution and suffering,
the prophets had all foretold that, but with it
would come the end of the age and the beginning
of the Good Times of the Messiah; and *he* would
be It.

In the light of modern psychology this was the
illusion of an unbalanced mind, and anything
Jesus said about it should be taken with reservations. This reference to the morbid side of the
mind of Jesus is necessary, however, because so
much has been made in Christianity of the Divinity of Jesus as based on his self-consciousness of
it, so much narrow minded bigotry and intolerance and cruel superstition has resulted from
the dogma that Jesus is the ' only-begotten Son
of God,' that it is well to remember that it has at

its base no firmer ground than the pathological egoism of an unbalanced mind.

There doubtless had been something of this simmering in the mind of Jesus before he went to John for baptism, but the great crowd, the strain of the emotional excitement, the shock of baptism, and especially the strange vision that came to him as he came up out of the water: the symbol of the dove and the voice saying, ' Thou art my Son, this day have I begotten you,' brought it all to a focus.

In the mind of Jesus, God was a Heavenly Father concerned in infinite love for each of his children. His Kingdom was not something that was to come in the future, it was present and always had been to those that had eyes to see and hearts willing to trust. The revelation of the kingdom was only delayed because as individuals they did not know it to be present and had not learned to trust its law of Love.

It was his mission, as he conceived it, to tell everyone the true nature of God's Kingdom, to proclaim its nearness, to persuade them to trust in it, and to conform their lives to its law of Love. Jesus did not openly proclaim his obsession that he was the Messiah — indeed it was pathetic to see how hard he tried not to do so — but all the time it was in his mind, to be revealed, as we have seen, when he became excited by opposition and crowd psychology.

It must be evident to all that there is the mingling of two very different lines of thought in the mind of Jesus: a psychopathic self-exaltation using his childish symbols of Messiah and judgment and the end of the age, and a clear and sane intuition of spiritual truth as it had come to him from association with the Essenes in the quiet of the Judean hills: God is Love; they that place their trust in Him and that love one another, will enter a freer and happier life process; and the Kingdom of Love, which is the Father's Kingdom, will be their Home now and for all eternity.

As the idea of the Kingdom of God is so fundamental in the saner mind of Jesus, it is well to consider it more at length. He never tired of talking about it, but he always half concealed it in parables. To Jesus the reality of the Kingdom was very true and vivid — often had he found refuge and solace in it — and it was precisely because it was so real to him that he could speak of it with eagerness and convincing authority. It was not to be an earthly kingdom in a social or political sense, and yet it was here and now. It is in the world but not of it; it is leaven, it is good seed, it is a treasure hid in a field, it is a pearl of great price for which a man may well sell all that he has to possess. Jesus says all of these things about it and many more, but he never says explicitly just what it is. Why did he do that?

The disciples asked him that very question, and he replied enigmatically: 'The secret of the Kingdom of Heaven is given to you, but to these outsiders it must be given in parables, so that for all their seeing they may not perceive, and for all their hearing they may not understand, lest they turn and be forgiven.' What was the reason that Jesus felt called to preach the nearness of the Kingdom of God and yet disguised it so that only the few would understand, and then felt discouraged and perplexed because they did not respond? It certainly had some clear meaning to himself, or he would not have talked about it so constantly and with such authority of conviction.

To Jesus the Kingdom was the polar opposite of the physical world that men are so generally satisfied with; it carried a spiritual significance, a freedom and release from bonds of body and matter. 'Except one be born from above he can not see the Kingdom of God. . . . That which is born of the flesh is flesh, that which is born of the Spirit is spirit.' It is only those who gain insight by cherishing love and simple faith who may enter into the happier and freer life that the Kingdom offers.

Let us go back to our suggestion that the early

Hasadim had come in contact with Buddhist missionaries, or at least with Buddhist teachings, which the Essenes cherished in an imperfect form among their secret teachings and ethical practices. Among these treasured teachings was something to do with cosmography, a description of the universe. If it was the common Jewish conception there would be no reason for keeping it secret; if it was Oriental or Buddhist, there most assuredly would be need for keeping it secret. What was the Buddhist cosmography? It consisted as we have seen, of a descending series of realms of existence: 1. Nirvana. 2. The realm of gods. 3. The realm of angels. 4. Conscious human life. 5. The animal world of perception. 6. The world of demons. 7. The nethermost hell, or world of ' hungry ' demons. Such a list as this was common among all Indians and Persians, and from them had been carried westward where it had affected the religious thought of many people. Among others it had appeared in the Apocryphal literature of Judea from the Third Century B. C. to the First Century A. D. In many instances the exact number had been lost and the distinctions blurred over. Among the Jews the list was, Heaven, the Angelic world, earth, sheol and hell. Among the Essenes these ideas of worlds and ranks of angels formed part of their secret teachings; and

they held peculiar ideas of fatality and predes-
tination and the universality of cause and effect,
and the movement of life from one plane of
existence to another.

The Buddhists, as we have seen, made much of
the impermanence of the body and soul and of
rebirths, not only on the earth plane but on all
other planes and from one plane to the next
higher, and of the part that Karma played in
the process. ‘ Make no mistake — God is not
mocked — a man will reap just what he sows;
he who sows for his flesh will reap destruction
from the flesh, and he who sows for the spirit
will reap life eternal from the Spirit,’ is Paul’s
echo of it. In the Buddhist idea this advance of
life from one plane to the next higher does not
necessarily take place at the time of death; as
we have seen, it is possible to achieve the first
enlightenment in the midst of the mortal life, as
did Gautama and the ‘ arahats.’ In this chain
of rebirths, the individual comes at last to a point
where rebirth on the physical plane ceases to
express the karmic idea and therefore ceases, all
further rebirths are on the angelic plane. In
later Buddhism this angelic plane is elaborated
as the Pure Land, and is pictured with all the
imagery of the Christian heaven.

Down to the Fifth Century B. C. when the
Jews came in contact with, Assyria and Persia,

they had no conception of the survival of the individual soul, nor of heaven. Gradually these views spread and were common in Jesus' day, but they differed from Buddhist ideas in always being objective and successive after death — a continuation of the earthly life in heaven.

Jesus' idea of the Kingdom of Heaven more nearly resembles the Buddist in that life in the Kingdom of Heaven might be here and now provided that the individual lived according to the law of the spirit world, that is, by love. It was a present and freer life of spirit, which lifted one above the turmoil and suffering of the mortal life. It was within, not without; it was present, it was now. Hence Jesus recognized that it would be useless to explain it in too great detail to those who were unready for its experience. They must first be awakened by his parables and hints of it, to a prior faith in it, to a prior desire for its benefits. When they reached that stage of spiritual life, they would understand by intuition its blessed and blissful reality.

This is precisely the Buddhist idea. Gautama grouped all thirst and its consequent clinging into three divisions of ' sankhara,' or processes of becoming: 1. The body with its sub-conscious instincts, sensations and perceptions. 2. The mental states. 3. The ' bodiless ' states. When the thirst and clinging of these three groups were overcome there would remain, over and above, the pure cognition of consciousness free of any and all consciousness of self. According to the teachings of Gautama, one would be living a physical life, an ' enlightened ' life, or a spiritual life, according as he had advanced in overcoming the corresponding groups of clinging. In the Sankhya philosophy there is the clear recognition of three ' gunas,' the physical, psychical and spiritual. In later Mahayana Buddhism the early belief in the intermediate realm of ' enlightenment ' is developed and emphasized as life in the Pure Land of Amitabha's Heaven.

It is not suggested that Jesus had any clear idea of these profound distinctions; it is only suggested that he had secured his idea of the Kingdom of Heaven from his contact in Essene circles with this ancient Buddhist cosmography, and had become convinced of its reality, as all Buddhists do, through his practice of meditation. It was his escape and refuge from the tormenting troubles of earthly life; its peace and tranquility was a refuge for his disordered mind; and, except when over-excited by great opposition and crowd psychology, enabled him to control his clinging to selfness and gain the wisdom and insight of its higher life. In this confidence and conviction Jesus was certainly a Buddhist at heart.

Because Jesus freely accepted invitations to hospitality offered by anyone, he was called, ' a wine-bibber and glutton.' And people condemned him for talking with publicans and prostitutes, but in both these things he was but following the example of Gautama who did the same with no fear of personal defilement, because it was the kind thing to do. And like the Buddhists he often retired to the solitude of the night and the hills for quiet meditation.

But especially was he a Buddhist in his attitude toward non-resistance. He is often reputed to be the original pacifist, but Christians have often interpreted his teachings as permitting the use of force in extreme circumstances. Of one thing, however, we may be certain, Jesus was no wavering politician. If he taught non-resistance at one time, he did to the end, with no exceptions or interpretations. Those who claim the contrary, appeal to two instances: cleansing the temple, and advising his disciples, on the road to Jerusalem, to purchase swords. The first is an instance of his erratic behavior under the influence of a hostile group psychology. But even then it is hard to believe that he, a single man, would venture to assault and drive out the many money changers and dealers in animals demanded by the temple sacrifices, who were intrenched in the favor of the temple au-

thorities by reason of the enormous profits they
derived from its monopoly. If he did it, it was
an insane thing to do. Probably Jesus was beside himself as he saw the desecration of ' his
Father's house,' and denounced it in no measured
terms. Very possibly he seized a small whip, or
a ' whip of small cords,' to emphasize his anger.
But there must have been something in the authority of his personality, something in their
sense of guilt, or the natural yielding to a half-
witted person, whose unreasoned anger is seen
to be futile. One can hardly, with reason, build
very much on this instance as fixing the sober
convictions of his calmer moments.

As to the second instance, there are strong
reasons for believing that the account in Luke
35; 35-38, is inaccurate. According to Moffatt's
translation, it reads:

And he said to them, ' When I sent you out with neither
purse, nor wallet, nor sandals, did you want for anything? '
' No,' they said, ' for nothing.' Then he said to them,
' But he who has a purse must take it now, and the same
with a wallet; and he who has no sword must sell his coat
and buy one. For I tell you this word of scripture must
be fulfilled in me: he was classed among criminals. Yet
there is an end to all that refers to me.' ' Lord,' they said,
' here are two swords.' ' Enough, enough! ' he answered.

This is so contrary to all of Jesus' other teachings, notably to his rebuke to Peter soon after,
who is reported to have resorted to its use. ' Put

up thy sword; he who appeals to the sword, shall perish by the sword.' It is easy to see reasons on the part of Luke for doubting in the face of the extreme danger that then confronted them, of any other advice than to provide arms for emergencies, hence the record as it stands. But how slight a change is necessary in the text to make the record harmonize with Jesus' otherwise uniform advocacy of non-resistance: simply the change in the form of one sentence from declarative to the form of a question. Then it would read:

And he said to them, 'When I sent you out with neither purse, nor wallet, nor sandals, did you want for anything?' 'No,' they said, 'for nothing.' Then he said to them, (Do you think I will advise any differently now? Do you think I will now say) he who has a purse must take it now, and the same with a wallet; and he who has no sword must sell his coat and buy one?'

The words that follow are a good instance of the many instances in the Gospels, where the writer, or editor, dresses up the narrative to tie it back to some Old Testament prophecy. But Jesus' words are again seen — as the disciples evidently fail to understand his meaning and call his attention to two swords that are at hand — as he wearily replies, 'Enough, Enough! (you have failed to understand me). In this form it makes the teachings consistent and reveals Jesus to have been a strict pacifist, like the Essenes and like all Buddhists.

Yes, in this as in all the teachings of Jesus we see only faith and trust in the power of Love. It is why Jesus is still the world's hope, in spite of the burden that Paul and the theologians have loaded upon him of philosophic theism and legalistic responsibility for sin, and mysteries of cult and ritual. It is not the Christ of Paul's theology that is the world's hope, it is Jesus' assertion and defense of Love as of the essence of the Divine Mind. And in estimating the genuineness of a man's trust in Love, there is nothing so searching as to examine his attitude toward non-resistance in the face of physical danger, and in the face of assaults, or fears of assault, on his will-to-power.

What then was there in the words of Jesus that made his friends forsake him, the authorities fear him, the Pharisees and Sadducees hate him and plot his death? It was because of his faith in Love, that led him to stand a pacifist in the face of his fellow Galilaean's militant and desperate patriotism; it was because he stood a socialist and a communist, denouncing the private possession of wealth as the root of all evil; that the rich Sadducees and the authorities feared him; it was because he stood a blasphemer and a heretic, in asserting his right as a son of God, to forgive sin, and to denounce Pharisees and Sadducees and High-priests alike for their hypocrisy and oppression, that they hated him and tried to put him to death. But the poor and the sick loved him for his revelation of ' truth in its beauty, love in its tenderness.'

The great parables of Jesus are all tinged with Buddhist thought and sentiment. The parable of the Good Samaritan denounced the selfish and hard hearted Pharisee and extolled the Buddhist kindness to the poor and sick. In the parable of the Prodigal Son the elder son pictures the common Jewish belief and the father's attitude is the typical Buddhist attitude of compassion and forgiveness and the resumption of spiritual relations. So also in the Great Commandments. It is Love for God, rather than the Jewish fear of Jehovah, that is commanded; it is love for the neighbor because in him is the same Buddha nature, rather than love for him in the same measure as one loves the self, which would be more after Jewish ideas.

The assertion of the nearness and accessibility of a present, freer life of spirit, and of the fundamental place that Love holds in its experience, especially as love is expressed in unselfish kindness and service between a man and his neighbor and as he illustrated it in his own willingness to die for love for others, these are the contributions of Jesus to the salvation of the world; and all these ideas are distinctly Buddhist rather than Jewish.

CHAPTER THIRTEEN

LATER CHRISTIANITY

IT IS not the purpose to make any extended reference to later and developed Christianity, but something must be said to bring out the difference between the actual teachings of Jesus and the Christianity of Paul and of later centuries.

The accounts of the crucifixion as given in Acts and Luke are evidently written by men who are intent on reproducing past conditions in a way to justify their present purposes and ideas and interests. More and more scholars are becoming convinced that the writers of Acts and the Gospels were deliberately covering up some serious divisions between the followers of John the Baptist and Jesus, and the gentile converts of Paul.

The account in Mark up to 16; 8, is generally accepted as the safest to go by. According to that, immediately at the arrest of Jesus the disciples returned to Galilee and resumed their former callings. Of the women who had ministered unto Jesus, the two Marys and Salome, at least, remained in Jerusalem, for very early on the following morning, it is doubtful if the legend of the ' third day ' can be true, they went to the tomb with spices and wrappings intending to embalm the body of Jesus for its permanent burial, but they found the tomb empty and the linen that Joseph had provided piled neatly as though it never had been used. As they went away from the tomb they met a young man clothed in white, the usual dress of an Essene brother, who told them that Jesus, the Nazoraean, i.e., the Essene, had risen from the dead, but had gone to Galilee where the disciples could meet him. Here the account in Mark ends.

The other accounts are later and show too many indications of editing to be reliable. Paul in his first letter to the Corinthians says that Peter was the first to meet Jesus after his crucifixion, and that the other disciples saw and talked with him later. They were convinced that Jesus had risen from the dead; of that there is no doubt. It is evident that Joseph of Arimathea had taken no one into his confidence, and that Jesus himself believed that he had actually risen from the dead. The disciples then returned to Jerusalem and formed a brotherhood after the pattern of the Essene brotherhoods except as to universal labor and the inclusion of women. Many think that the earliest members came largely from the Essenes. There are still no signs of any purpose to form a new sect or church; they are good and loyal Jews, bound together in fellowship because of a common acceptance of Love as the way of life, and buoyed up by a common faith in Jesus as being the Messiah.

As to their earliest beliefs, three things stand out clearly: 1. They believed in the resurrection of the dead and in the Messiahship of Jesus. This was the basis of their first preaching; they said little as to the call to repentance as a preparation for the coming of the Kingdom: Jesus was risen, The Kingdom was here, Jesus was the Messiah! As to the meaning of the Kingdom of God the early followers certainly misunderstood it, for they built their faith on a second coming of Jesus to establish it, and the believers, in power and glory. 2. They believed themselves to be entrusted with a message of salvation in his name, and to be divinely inspired for its proclamation exactly as were the prophets of old, and as Jesus had been. 3. They believed in the communistic principles of the Essenes.

At this same time there were many followers of John the Baptist, with whom there was mutual sympathy, and yet with whom there were some differences. The followers of John were more typical Jews, they were more punctilious in observing the Mosaic code and observing the rites; but both groups at first believed that salvation was for the Jews primarily and if gentiles were converted they must first become proselytes.

The followers of Jesus, while still considering themselves good Jews, were more liberal in their attitude toward the gentiles, they avoided the temple and its bloody sacrifices, but attended the synagogs and observed the ordinary rites. In addition they believed that Jesus was the Messiah, while the followers of John only gradually came to that belief. The followers of Jesus, believing him to be the Messiah and to have risen from the dead, apparently gave up all productive labor and lived for the time on their capital, expecting daily the second coming of Jesus in power and glory. In addition the followers of Jesus were steadily making converts from among the Greek Jews and the gentiles, who naturally cared less or nothing for the Mosaic rites. They had become liberalized and were neglecting and often ignoring observances that the orthodox Jews held to be essential. As a consequence, in a very short time, there was friction between them. A sample of how irritating these liberal ideas might be is seen in Peter's words at Pentecost. While the followers of John remained in Jerusalem, apparently on good terms with the authorities of the Temple, the followers of Jesus were soon being persecuted and scattered abroad. It is significant, that in this persecution the first recorded victim was Stephen, a Greek, and his persecutors were strict Pharisees.

The followers of Jesus and of John the Baptist gradually drew together. At first Peter was the head of the followers of Jesus, but after the persecution, James, the so-called ' brother of the Lord,' who was an Essene follower of John at first, appears to have become the leader of the united groups.

With the coming of Paul a new condition of affairs arose. Paul had his vision of a risen Christ within three or four years (perhaps much longer) of the crucifixion of Jesus, and at that time he was interested in the persecutions of the followers of Jesus. He felt called to carry his new faith in Jesus as the risen Christ, to the gentiles, and very early they claimed exemption from the Mosaic code. This resulted in a cleavage between the Jewish followers of John and Jesus, and the gentile Christians. This increased seriously and finally came to an open rupture between the two factions. Peter at first wavered between the two, but finally cast in his lot with the gentile Christians as far as this exemption was concerned, and there is reason to believe that he devoted his life to missionary work in Europe exactly as did Paul, although nothing is said of it in Acts, which, in its latter part is exclusively devoted to the fortunes of Paul. Apparently Peter and Paul differed to the last in their conception of the person of Jesus; Peter believed

him to be a human exalted to be the Messiah;
Paul believing him to be Divine who emptied
himself of his divine attributes. Later Peter
evidently made his way to Rome and there gathered a group of converts which afterward became the most important church of all, although
nothing is said of it in Acts.

The gentile Christian Church under Paul's
able leadership soon became an important institution, with distinctive doctrines and message.
There is no longer the simple call to repentance,
faith in Jehovah and the Mosaic ritual of purity.
It took on very important elements of Greek
philosophy, and mystic speculations of savior-
gods and ceremonials, from the dominant mystery religions of the Roman Empire. Especially
did they find themselves in competition with the
worship of Mithra, a Persian Sun-god, and were
obliged to adopt much of their ritual and ideas
to satisfy the demands of the gentile world. Into
this complex blending of philosophy and mysticism, went an exaggeration of the legends of
Jesus' birth, self-consciousness of Divinity, miracles, resurrection and ascension.

The vital difference in their attitude toward
the person of Jesus lay in this: the followers of
John and Jesus looked upon Jesus as an historical person who had been annointed with
power by the Holy Spirit to be the Messiah and

the Savior of the world. The gentile Christians, followers of Paul, looked upon Jesus as the Divine Son of God, who had emptied himself of his Divine attributes to be born of a virgin, and by his death on the cross, symbolic of the Pascal lamb, to have made atonement for the sin of the world.

In addition to this doctrinal difference there were two others of great importance. John had said, ' There cometh after me, he that is mightier than I, the latchet of whose shoes I am not worthy to stoop down and unloose. I baptised you with water; but he shall baptise you with the Holy Spirit.' John's baptism was a cleansing from sin and a sign of repentance. Jesus and his followers did little or no baptism. After Pentecost when the Holy Spirit was bestowed with power, the Apostles conferred it upon believers and converts by the laying on of hands. It was conceived of as the Divine spirit confering supernatural gifts of power, healing, tongues, teaching, etc. This was not an initiation because the Apostles did not at first think of forming a new sect.

Paul, on the other hand, was acquainted with the initiation rites of the mystery religions of the Greek world, and the formula and procedure which he instituted and which later became the practice of the Christian Church, consisted of baptism, generally by sprinkling, with the laying on of hands, and the formula, at first, ' in the name of Jesus.' Later as the distinction of the Holy Spirit as the third person of the Trinity became developed, the triune formula, ' in the name of the Father, Son, and Holy Spirit,' was adopted and, with the gradual union of the three groups, became the general practice of the Christian Church. These doctrinal differences, namely, as to the person of Jesus, as to the nature of the Holy Spirit, and as to the meaning and practice of baptism, served to divide and embitter for centuries the factions of the early Christian Church.

The gentile followers of Paul were centered at Antioch and soon came to be called Christians. There were many Petrine groups in Asia Minor and Europe, but gradually the influence of Paul won them over to his way of thinking. The group that held off the longest, probably, was the one at Rome. This important group was not entirely won over until long after the death of both Paul and Peter, in the middle of the Second Century. Before that time the followers of Peter and the followers of Paul had worshipped in separate groups and there are hints in some of the early writings of violent quarrels between them. It was not until the time of Anicetus, who was the head of the Petrine group in 150

A.D. whom Polycarp was able to convince as to the reasonableness of the Pauline doctrines, that the breach was healed.

The gradual union of the three groups in Jerusalem is seen in the leadership of James, a follower of John the Baptist, over the Jewish followers of the Apostles; and the addition of the Seven Deacons, who were leaders of the Pauline gentile Christians, to be leaders of the united body of believers together with the Apostles and Paul. The growing Church, in time, demanded more information about the earthly life of Jesus, and the leaders were anxious to cover up as well as they could the earlier divisions among them, hence the Gospels and Acts with all their editing and rationalizing and addition of myths and legends, and conformity to prophecy.

In the years that followed the great teachers and saints added refinements and interpretations without end; and the great councils of Bishops adopted creeds and judged as to what was orthodox and what it was heresy to believe. It must be noticed, that the doctrines that survived had little to do with the ideas of Jesus and had very much to do with the theistic ideas of Paul. Very often that was declared to be orthodox that supported and increased the authority of the Church as a centralized institution and hierarchy, and that was heteradox which tended toward indi-

vidualism and free will. This went on until the
Fifteenth Century when, under the leadership of
Luther, the Reformation divided the Church,
into Catholic, which held to the authority of a
centralized Mother-Church, and Protestants
who believed in salvation by individual faith
based on the inspiration of the Bible. Besides
the Roman Catholic Church built on the authority of the Pope at Rome, there is the Greek Catholic and the Gregorian Catholic.

Protestants are divided into scores of sects,
often with slight differences, divided as to
whether they accept all or a part of the teachings
of Luther, Calvin, Wesley, Knox, or Mary
Baker Eddy; or who emphasize particular things
as baptists, adventists, psychologists, etc. In a
general way the Protestant Church may be divided into two great divisions: fundamentalists
and modernists. The beliefs of fundamentalists
are nearer together than the beliefs of modernists and can be stated more precisely. For instance the China Inland Mission is an inter-de-
nominational society. They publish the following statement which will do very fairly for all
fundamentalists:

1. The divine inspiration and consequent authority of
the whole canonical Scriptures.
2. The doctrine of the Trinity.
3. The fall of man, his consequent moral depravity
and his need of regeneration.

4. The atonement through the substitutionary death of Christ.

5. The doctrine of justification by faith.

6. The resurrection of the body, both in the case of the just and the unjust.

7. The eternal life of the saved and the eternal punishment of the lost.

One notices in the above the entire absence of the particular things that Jesus emphasized, namely, the Kingdom of Heaven, the Law of Love, and voluntary poverty.

It is not so easy to make a brief statement as to the general belief of modernists, for having forsaken such a strict and definite creed as the foregoing, there is room for wide differences.

More and more do modernists drift away from Paul's theistic and legalistic dogmatism, toward the freedom of Jesus' ethical idealism. For instance a writer in Hibbert Journal, J. S. MacKenzie, (Jan. 1926) writes:

It is here that the true meaning of the Holy Spirit becomes especially apparent; and it is on the appropriation and development of the Spirit that the hopes of the world now mainly rest . . . . It has been this conception (God as Love, Wisdom, and Creative Activity), more or less explicitly recognized, of the Divine element in human life — the Spirit of Love as its foundation and the Spirit of Wisdom and Creative Activity as enabling us to devise and apply methods of understanding and co-operation.

That is, for modernist Christians, the idea of a transcendent, personal God, is universalized into

a personalized and immanent Divinity conceived
of as Love, Wisdom and Creative Activity; while
the Risen Christ is merged into the Holy Spirit
of Love.

Christians who have been brought up on the
accounts of the early beginnings of Christianity
as given in the Gospels and Acts, little comprehend how vast was the influence of John the Baptist in the subsequent history of Eastern Christianity. John left many disciples who at an early
date joined with the conservative Jewish followers of Jesus to be the founders of what is com-
monly known as Gnostic Christianity. All we
know about it from the account given in Acts
and in Paul's letters are the scattered references
to it as gnostic heresies that must be denounced.

Eastern Christianity was a strange mingling
of John's Judaism and his particular teachings
concerning repentance and baptism and a life of
purity, and belief that Jesus was the Messiah,
together with obscure ideas of Babylonian and
Persian gnostic dualism. At an early date this
eastern type of Christianity divided itself into
many different sects known as the Disciples of
John the Baptiser, Nestorians, Mandæans,
Manichæans, Mandelians, etc. Late discoveries
in Central Asia are revealing the amazing fact
that these gnostic forms of Christianity grew

faster in Asia, during the first four centuries, than did the Pauline type of philosophic theism spread in Europe and northern Africa. By the Fifth Century there are now thought to have been not less than ten million believers.

To show how far Nestorian and Manichæan Christianity had extended, a quotation is here made from a very early Chinese work.

In a Buddhist work published (in China) a few years after the erection of the Nestorian tablet, it has been discovered by a modern Japanese scholar that the Christian priest Adam collaborated with an Indian Buddhist monk named Prejna, in the translation of a Buddhist sutra — and received an imperial snub for his pains. 'The Emperor (Te-Tsung, 780-804 A. D.) who was intelligent, wise and accomplished, who revered the canon of the Shakya (Gautama), examined what they had translated, and found that the principles contained in it were obscure and the wording was diffuse. Moreover, the Sangharama (monastery) of the Buddhists and the monastery of the Nestorians differ much in their customs, and their religious practices being entirely opposed to each other, Adam handing down the teachings of the Messiah, while the Shakya scholars propagate the sutras of the Buddha. It is to be wished that the boundaries of the doctrines may be kept distinct and their followers may not intermingle. Orthodoxy and Heterodoxy are different things, just as the rivers King and Wei have a different course.' — (*Saeki.*)

It was only the combined persecutions of Islam in the rear, Chinese nationalism in front, and Hindu impenetrability cutting off any escape, that the spread of Gnostic Christianity was checked and finally destroyed. All this vast religious life was founded on John the Baptist rather than on Jesus or Paul.

And in Europe, it was not so much the political Messianism of the Jews, or the ethical ideals of Jesus, that prevailed, as it was the philosophized interpretation of them that came to the master mind of Paul in the years that followed his vision of the Risen Christ. The Christian idea of the relation of the Risen Christ to the Kingdom of God, considered simply as the rule of God in human hearts and human affairs, carries with it many of the ideas of Jesus, to be sure, but in the main as expressed in theology and institutions, Christianity is far more of Paul than it is of Jesus.

Concerning the conception of the Kingdom of God, which Jesus made so prominent, there is almost no evidence of an understanding of it, or interest in it, by the Christian Church. In a general way it was considered to be synonomous with the Church, visible and invisible. Paul showed but slight knowledge or interest in it. The great councils, in formulating the creeds tell us nothing about it. Modern catechisms only say that baptised believers become members of it. In the modern emphasis on ethical idealism, and the common fear of mysticism, men see the Kingdom in some vague way as the idealized social community. Only to the great mystics of the

Church has the vision of Jesus in this particular been preserved. And Jesus' faith in the supremacy of Love, while held in theory, is often forgotten in the Christian's larger interest in theistic dogmas, competitive economics and private profit, nationalism and war.

CHAPTER FOURTEEN

LATER BUDDHISM

FOR THE first three hundred years after the death of Gautama, Buddhism developed almost unhindered from outside religions. Only very gradually did the influence of Hindu Vedantism begin to show effect.

The Upanishads developed within Vedantism the idea of the neuter impersonal Brahman (Atman), conceived of as the sole and All-inclusive Reality, which to cognition is *not so, not so.* Buddhism apparently never understood this, and blindly opposed itself to Brahma, conceived of as a masculine individuality existing in the realm of the gods, the realm next below Nirvana, where he was subject to the universal law of causation. At the same time the Buddhist conception of the Dharmakaya is indistinguishable from the Vedanta Brahman.

After all there is not much difference in the background of these two great religions. If the question, ' What must I do to be saved? ' were asked of each, they would both answer, ' Overcome the illusion of selfness, by the restraint of desire.' Vedantists would achieve the result by yoga practice and meditative speculations; while

Buddhists would achieve it by living up to an ethical way of life that is designed to root it out. The affinity of Jesus to Buddhism is seen in the reply that he would make to the same question, ' Go sell all that thou hast and give to the poor, and thou shalt have treasure in heaven and come take up thy cross and follow me.' ' He that loseth his life, shall save it.'

The Council of Asoka revealed serious internal differences which were deepened rather than composed by it. At first Buddhists deprecated metaphysical discussion, but after this council they more and more yielded to its lure. After that date primative, or Hinayana Buddhism, as it came to be called, continued in India and spread to Burmah and Ceylon, while the movement northward, coming in contact, as it did, with virile religions like Persian Mazdæism and Babylonian gnostic and mystery cults, and later in contact with Christian Gnostic sects, was profoundly influenced by them; the new type of Buddhism becoming known as the Mahayana, the ' larger, or more inclusive, vehicle.' The effect upon Buddhism as it moved northward into Central Asia and came into contact with these more theistic and gnostic sects, was to change the primative type into one far more philosophic and speculative. By the time of the great Coun-

cil called by Kanishka about the close of the
First Century A.D. and with the appearance
of Ashvagosha, these internal differences became definite. Ashvagosha was a Brahmin by
birth, and wandered about India seeking knowledge; eventually he settled at Benares and came
to have great renown for his poetry, wide scholarship and ability as a controversalist. For some
unknown reason he became converted to Buddhism of the Hinayana type. As a Buddhist
monk he became noted for his sanctity. India
at that time was in a tumult of a desperate resistance to conquest by a Scythian emperor
named Kanishka. When this emperor captured
Benares, he is said to have promised to spare the
city if Ashvagosha was given him for a hostage,
and he be given the possession of Buddha's begging bowl. His request was granted and Ashvagosha was taken north to Central Asia, to the
capitol of the largest strictly Buddhist empire in
history. There at the cross roads of Europe and
Egypt and India and China, Ashvagosha became
acquainted with the philosophies and religions of
the West. He comes to appreciate the deficien-
cies of the primitive Hinayana and thinks out a
fuller interpretation of the Buddha's teachings.

Ashvagosha was to Buddhism what Origin was
to Christianity: they each supplied a metaphysic

that made worship possible. By doing so, Ashvagosha laid the foundation for all the vast superstructure of Northern Buddhism, with its divergent speculations and scores of sects, its hundred gods and ranks of Buddhas and Bodhisattvas.

There is no doubt but what Ashvagosha was brought to his advanced interpretation of Gautama's teachings by his contact with the same gnostic teachings from Persia and Babylonia which, in the west and at the same time, were influencing Christianity. Compare, for instance the words of the author of John's Gospel, which he places in the mouth of Jesus, ' I and the Father are One,' and Origin's distinction of God as Heavenly Father, God as the Risen Christ, and the Divine nature of the historic Jesus; with Ashvagosha's deification of Gautama and his appearances as Essence-body (Buddahood), Bliss-body (Heavenly manifestation as Buddha), and Incarnation-body (the earthly Gautama).

Then compare the Logos doctrine of the author of John's Gospel with the Mahayana Dharmakaya, considered not as a personal being but as the Womb-of-All, that in its totality changes not, but appears in endless manifestations of gods and monks and poor people and geniuses and arts and cultures, and worlds and flowers and sufferers in lowest hells. This Dharmakaya is the beneficent ground of All, from which emanates, also, in more particular self expression, the Buddhas and Bodisattvas on their missions of enlightenment and compassion. Later on the Dharmakaya takes on a more personal form as Adi-Budda and his six-fold appearance in particular Buddhas, of which eventually Amitaba is most highly honored and Kwanyin most deeply beloved. But in whatever form the Dharmakaya is revealed, in its essence it is always the same undifferentiated ocean of Light and Life and Love. It is the privilege of all animate life, as they become able by disciplined desire to throw off one by one the limitations and bonds of ignorance, and lust and clinging to self-ness, to unfold into its unified, harmonious Nirvana.

All of this was not given by Ashvagosha, of course, but was developed by scores of great teachers and scholars, of whom we mention especially, Nargajuna, who followed very soon after, and the brothers Asanga and Vasabandhu.

About the Fifth Century, in the great Han Dynasty, we find the first sure contact in China of Buddhism and Christianity in both its Nestorian and Manichæan forms. Apparently they have been in friendly contact for some time; they have similar names: Buddhism is called the

Great Sun Religion, and Christianity is called the Luminous Religion, which in Chinese characters is a combination of the former. So close is the intimacy, that we find their leaders going to each other for instruction and collaboration in translations.

Different sects of Buddhists in China and Japan drive through recorded lists of 'Patriarchs' from widely different religious backgrounds. In the Tantrik Buddhism of Tibet and Mongolia we see an out-cropping of the most ancient cults of animism and demon worship with vestiges of phallic worship, that had revealed itself in earlier times in ancient India and Chaldæa and Egypt and even in the early days of the Hebrews. In China the great sect of the Chan Buddhists who placed emphasis on direct spiritual insight, derived from the disciplinary and meditative sects of India. In Japan, the Shingon sect derives from teachers acquainted with Egyptian and Indian practices of esoteric magic and gnostic secrets; the Zen sect, like the Chan, makes much of Indian yoga practices and meditation. In the Yodo and the Shinshu sects with their characteristic ' salvation by faith in Amida's Vow,' we see the influence of this friendly contact of Buddhists and Christians in Central Asia and in China which we have just noticed.

Amida, it is said, has two qualities by which he saves us: Mercy and Wisdom. We, sentient beings, travail in pain, being fast bound in a kind of slavery to sin and evil; and from this we can not free ourselves because the fetters have been fastened on us by Karma of an immemorial past, And Karma has relations not only with the past; it affects our present condition, it brings with it an endless chain of rebirth, life and death, which stretch away into the boundless future. From this bondage Amida delivers us. He looseth the bonds of sin and evil by the might accruing to him by his great vow, and by his light he illuminates our minds, giving us supernatural and glorious wisdom. Of his mercy he places us in a position equal to his own, practically giving us power to become ' sons of God.' — (*Lloyd's Shinran and His Work.*)

An interesting differentiating of the different Buddhist sects in modern Japan is given by Jisogi, in a pamphlet entitled, The Influence of Buddhism on Japanese National Ideals. He writes:

In other sects of Japanese Buddhism, religious rites and observances are practised for the sake of the benefit accruing to the worshippers therefrom. Thus the Shingon of Tendai devotee recites mandares and Dharani, or goes through manual acts in order, by some thurgic process to compel the deity to do what he, the worshipper, happens to desire.

Thus the disciple of Zen sits absorbed in contemplation, waiting for the moment when the Divine Light shall break into his soul, and the Divine Voice speak to his conscience with an illuminative power that defies description, and in words that can not be uttered or pronounced.

Thus, even the pious believer of the Jodo sect recites his ' nembutsu ' with fervent zeal, believing that with every repetition of the Divine Name, and every moving of the beads of his rosary, he adds to his own stock of merit, and makes his calling and election sure.

But, for the Shin sect believer, the church going and religious observances assume a different aspect. Here there is no question of acquiring God's favor, or obtaining a benefit. Everything has already been obtained that the soul can possibly wish for. It only remains for the individual to continually give thanks to Buddha for 'his inestimable gift.' The more the value of that gift is appreciated at its proper worth, the more fervent and constant will be the expression of the believer's gratitude. Hence it is that the whole sum of the religious observances of the believers of the Shin sect, after conversion, may be expressed in the one word, ' ho-on,' the giving of thanks always.

The sacred literature of Buddhism is enormous. In a recent list there are over fourteen thousand titles of sutras, shastras, and vinaya. Some are original teachings of Gautama, some are later but are ascribed to him. Then there are commentaries and commentaries on commentaries.

Some of them are very voluminous, one in its unabridged form consisted of over 100,000 couplets. In the life of Yuen-chuang, a famous Chinese Buddhist scholar, it is stated that just before his death he completed a translation of an abridged form of the Prajnapariminta sutra in 600 chapters, in 102 volumes. No Buddhist scholar ever ' knows ' them all; some know ten, some twenty, some fifty, but very few know a hundred.

The outstanding sutras of modern Buddhism are the Lotus of the Perfect Law which shows remarkable likeness to the Gospel of John in its emphasis on the Divine nature revealing itself in Life, Light and Love. This sutra is used by nearly all modern sects. The Diamond sutra is also widely used, and the Meditation sutra. The Awakening of Faith, said to have been written by Ashvagosha, develops the doctrine of salvation by faith in Amitabha and is used by all the Amitabha sects. It shows acquaintance with the same oriental mystery-religions from which Christianity drew its idea of a savior-god. The Garland of Jatakas, or birth stories of the Buddha, is written in the very best Sanskrit poetry by Aryasura and retells ancient legends with homiletic intent.

At present there is a strong tendency in the Buddhism of Japan, especially among the ' salvation by faith ' Amida sects, to adopt Christian methods of administration, namely, centralized organization, publicity and magazines, colleges and universities, educated priesthood over parish temples, lay associations of young men, clubs and classes for boys and girls, weekly worship and preaching, Sunday-schools and revival meetings. This is true to a less degree in China, also, and indicates a slow drawing together of the two great religions.

CHAPTER FIFTEEN

CHRISTIAN AND BUDDHIST CONTRASTING IDEAS OF SELF

THERE is one idea in Christianity that is quite contrary to the corresponding one in Buddhism, namely, the Christian idea of an immortal soul as contrasted with the Buddhist doctrine of an impermanent selfhood. In our study of the life of Jesus we saw that he urged a decided restraint of desire; in fact, his attitude in this regard is so like the Buddhist attitude as to impress one as having had a like origin. Jesus repeatedly said that if any one was to be his disciple he must forsake wealth and lands, and even wife and family if necessary. He was to take no thought for the morrow, what he was to eat or wear, which is precisely the rule that Gautama gave his disciples. Even in Jesus' obsession that he was the Messiah, there is a similarity to the Buddhist ideas of Enlightenment and Nirvana.

But from the day that Paul's influence and teachings began to dominate Christianity, it has soft-pedaled restraint of desire and has stressed the idea and immortal value of the individual soul. In Paul's system, man is conceived as born in sin because of the original sin of Adam, besides being guilty of his own sins, and, therefore must surely die. To meet this situation, Paul adopted a current pagan idea of a savior-god and developed the theistic idea that Jesus was the only-begotten Son of God, whose death on the cross was an atonement for the sin of the whole world, and which was available to all who placed their faith in his atoning sacrifice.

The idea that God could so love the world as to give his only-begotten Son to be a ransom for sinners, placed so extraordinary a valuation on the souls of men, involved their eternal existence, and made so important their future destiny whether in bliss or torment, that the earlier idea of the Jews—and fundamentally, of Jesus also —that the grave ordinarily ended all, was quickly abandoned and forgotten. From Paul's time on, the idea of an immortal soul as an essential part of Christian belief has been working out its demoralizing effects.

In contrast to this we place Gautama's insistence that any idea of a permanent selfhood, of a particular I, or mine, is an illusion of ignorance that must be gotten rid of at all costs.

In the later histories of Buddhism and Christianity we may see how these opposing conceptions have worked out in social results. We boast of our Christian civilization as being the last word in culture, oblivious to the fact that its

crowning achievement is a world war, and that
it is still working out into individual discontent
and injustice, and into social and political chaos.

Christianity has had an exclusive influence
over the civilization of Europe for fifteen hundred years and has made Christian nations characteristically intolerant, proud, aggressive, selfish, domineering and thoughtless. Part of this,
no doubt, is due to the fact that Christianity has
developed among Teutonic, Mediterranean,
Slavic and Semitic races, who are naturally voli-
tional and given over to the will-to-power.
Nevertheless, it has tended through the centuries
to develop an ever increasing individualism.

Christianity has not acted as a restraint on
this, but has intensified it, making Christian nations rich, strong, aggressive, nationalistic, given
to an exaggeration of alleged rights and vested
interests; ever tending toward quarrels, rebel-
lions, invasions and wars innumerable. And all
this in spite of the fact that their religion pro-
fesses to be the religion of the Prince of Peace.

Who can honestly view the present state of
affairs in rich and educated and Christian America with pride? Venality common among our
high officials, an acceptance of gross disorder
and violence as inevitable, a conniving at the
breaking of laws that we do not like, the presence of great organizations devoted to the violent

enforcement of individual purposes, the employment of vast wealth to condition political results,
the avaricious greed of doctors and lawyers, the
illegal combinations to enforce monopolies and
unjust prices, open suppression of civil liberties
and free speech, the feverish desire for more and
more sensual satisfactions, the license of young
people in sex relations, open eroticism in literature, art and the drama, the universal presence
of avarice, noise, rush and strain, the general demand for entertainment, distraction, travel, excitement; jazz music taking the place of melody,
the fox trot and charleston taking the place of the
minuet and folk-dance, the raucous radio usurp-
ing the time for reading and quiet meditation, the
rush of motor trips for leisurely rest. Exaggeration of selfness is at the root of it all! Our
whole civilization is an apotheosis of self-seeking.
Our economics are founded on legalized selfishness. The private holding of wealth with the
power it gives over others, is the great desidera-
tum, and private profit, the only recognized motive; and force and preparedness the only ground
of confidence that it will continue. Shame on
Christianity for its part in developing such an
unworthy and so disgraceful a civilization. Nor
can Christianity rightly evade its responsibility,
for its attitude toward the individual, its exaggeration of self, lies at the root of it all.

It is often said that Christianity should not be blamed for this, because the teachings of Jesus have not honestly been tried. This is exactly true, but when the teachings of Jesus are tried it will not be a modified form of Christianity, but will be Buddhism, pure and simple. And the resulting civilization will be Buddhist and not Christian.

On the other hand Buddhism developed among oriental races who are temperamentally more thoughtful and easy going. Buddhism satisfied their natural will-to-live, and in its turn, intensified it to make them characteristically peace-loving, intellectual, paternalistic and socially-minded. They seem to more energetic Europeans to be lazy and inert and selfish; just as Europeans seem to them to be self-centered, egoistic, thoughtless, materialistic and hard to get along with. Buddhism has certainly tended in the direction of a richer enjoyment of living and to the development of a more meditative and thoughtful habit, that is often accompanied by a willingness to live according to the law of least resistance and, as far as social conditions are concerned, to let well enough alone.

It is interesting to contemplate how things have worked out in these two great religions. Christianity places first emphasis on doctrines and creeds and intellectual beliefs, but is thoughtless and irrational. Buddhism places first emphasis on love for all animate life, but is content to cherish the spirit of love and to neglect its expression in pragmatic institutions for social welfare. Buddhism is essentially a practical way of life, but Buddhist scholars have given far more thought to the implications of life and death than have Christian scholars. And, on the contrary, Christianity which is essentially concerned with the legalistic relations of the soul to the Divine Judge, has given more attention to the application of their religion to social institutions.

Modern Christianity and modern Buddhism are great trees that have grown from small seed, in whose branches national cultures and civilizations have built their nests. It is futile to look for figs on thistles or expect to gather grapes from thorn bushes. If we are to hope for better fruit we must go back to the simple, but vital, truths of Gautama and Jesus; we must cross fertilize and plant new seed.

If the ideas of Jesus are ever to be given a fair trial, certain values must be given a more important place and conserved, and certain defects of modern Christianity and modern Buddhism must be eliminated. In these days a religion to be universal must be rational and scientific and appeal to the highest spiritual insight and ideals. It must not be much given to creeds or dogma, or to authority; it must be rational and tolerant and elastic, willing to learn from the unfolding experience of the man on the street as well as from the scientist and the philosopher. It must be willing to appreciate the good elements of other religions and willing to adopt them—in this case to adopt the rationality of Buddhism and the practical social service of Christianity. In particular a religion to be of service to our own day must free itself from all alliance with, or dependence on the present acquisitive and competitive system of economics. It must abandon the present conventional attitude of the Christian church in the matter of the private holding of property. If it is to exalt the principle of Love, it must trust Love to be the basis of its economics; it must so favor co-operation and equal participation that the poor and the socialists and communists will look to it as their kind of religion. The practice of Gautama and the Buddhist monks and of the Essene brotherhoods and of Jesus in this regard must be recovered and adapted to present day and future needs.

The present conventional attitude of religion toward the sex problem must also be changed. Paul's teaching and example in this regard is one of the worst blots on Christian history. For two thousand years it has forced on a large portion of the world the illusion that there is something sacred about celibacy, and there is something carnal and wicked about sex-love. Nothing could be more contrary to biological facts. The advantages of a monogamic marriage of true love is too self evident to be questioned, but if true love departs, or was never present, the speedy ending of unhappy marriages must be made simple and honorable.

While Jesus followed the celibate rule of the Essene brotherhood, he in no sense gave ground for Paul's drastic condemnation of sex as carnal and wicked. Jesus' attitude toward women, even toward prostitutes, was always one of kindness and respect. Gautama warned against the illusion of lust and rightly, but he recognized marriage as honorable and provided for it in lay membership. A later authority recommends that young men first enter the married life before attempting the homeless life of the monks. Among the Essene brotherhoods there was a second order of married brothers, and the modern Shinshu sect in Japan encourages the marriage of monks. And the whole experience of the protestant clergy is in favor of marriage.

As the basis for a synthetic religion nothing could be better than Gautama's Four Noble Truths and his Golden Path. Milleniums of experience have proven beyond all cavil that they lead toward purity of individual life and the steady improvement of society and the state. Because of the advantage which we have by our knowledge of science, we may think it better to use other words for their cosmography.

1. The atomic plane. 2. The plane of protoplasmic bacteria. 3. The sensitive plane of vegetable life. 4. The perceptive plane of animal life. 5. Conscious plane of human life. 6. The psychic plane of living ideas. 7. The spiritual plane of undifferentiated participation in Truth and beauty. On all these planes we know that life has been functioning, is functioning now, and forever will function in an interweaving complex of action, reaction and interaction, in a never ending process and progress from one plane of existence to another, and in eternal recurrence.

Gautama's Golden Path has the merit of offering a practical and reasonable method for attaining this advancement within the short span of mortal life. It is open to trial and demonstration, carries its own proof, and accomplishes the result in a way by which ' things do not have to be done over again.' First get rid of the pernicious idea that the ego-self is of any permanent significance, or its desires of any inherent importance; only then will there be any hope for the individual and general increase of happiness

and advancement, for happier and more successful homes, for a more brotherly and more just
system of economics, and for the development of
a wiser, kinder, and more auspicious culture and
civilization.

This can all be brought about if we are willing
to follow Gautama's rule of life in the spirit of
unselfish love as taught by Jesus.

CHAPTER SIXTEEN

CHRISTIAN AND BUDDHIST AGREEMENT THAT LOVE IS ULTIMATE REALITY

As we have seen, Gautama emphasized the universality of a law of causation which was called Karma. Such a thing as a Jehovah God punishing whom he will, forgiving whom he will, rewarding whom he will, leaving each thing and each soul at the mercy of divine caprice and election, is inconceivable where Karma rules. Such a law, standing by itself is heartless and pessimistic. It is in the further conception, that Gautama adds, that back of Karma is an Ultimate Principle to which it must conform and by which its blind energy is gradually changed to life, to sensation, to perception, to consciousness, to meaning and idea, to spirit and significance, to the supremely loving intelligence of an harmonious and unified Wholeness. This All-inclusive Wholeness he called the Dharmakaya, the Body of Love and Truth; and its Ultimate Principle he called, Love. Jesus followed Gautama in emphasizing Love as the essence of the Divine Nature and Love as the all-pervading Law and Spirit of his Creation.

Love saves Karma from its otherwise heartless determinism. For if evil and selfish acts bring retribution then good and unselfish acts and desires bring corresponding rewards; and if there are other worlds and freer and purer lives than this, Karma over-ruled by Love will ultimately bring release from this and participation in that. It is an illusion of ignorance that keeps one from trusting Karma, from realizing the evanescence of worldly things, that leads one to cling so tenaciously to sensual comforts, alluring ideas, and the intoxication of selfness, only to suffer because that clinging compels rebirth into old conditions on the old planes.

If Love-controlled Karma is trusted and obeyed, the grip and clinging and fire of earthly desires, if unfed by the fuel of lust and ideation and selfhood, will burn itself out at the long last, and a truer self—not the conscious empirical self —will emerge of its physical and therefore impermanent and changing body-form, into a state where following rebirths will be on a higher plane of psychical and spiritual reality.

Jesus followed Gautama in this faith. But for a Christian to give up his faith in his independent selfhood and its dear hope of immortality with friends about the throne of God, seems like giving up all that makes life bearable. Here is where the doctrine of an impermanent soul becomes so perplexing and confusing for most

Christians. They can understand how an eternal soul can partake of future bliss, or think they can, but how an impermanent soul that comes to an end with the death of the body, can partake of future bliss, is incomprehensible. The Christian at once thinks, ' If my conscious soul comes to an end with the death of the body, how can I have any hope of Heaven?' Well, the ' I ' that the Christian has in mind can not, but to the Buddhist the conscious I is not the true self. To the Buddhist the conscious I to which the Christian clings so tenaciously, is but the ripple on the surface of some boundless ocean—thrown up by some wind of creative activity—and conditioned as to its appearance and qualities by its particular karma at the moment of birth, and which karma will itself be affected by the use one makes of his transient life, to condition all future ripples of rebirth in his series. After coming by intuition to see the freedom of the Buddha-nature that is the goal of his present denial of the illusions of the senses, the mental processes and of the idea of a personal selfhood, death appears not so much as a release from the hard conditions of mortality for himself, as the ending of a chain of rebirths into those conditions of earthly suffering for innumerable others. He sees, also, that all the innumerable appearances which have preceded his appearance under this particular karmic-cycle, are being enlightened and gaining their freedom in him and through him. As the Christian writer in the book of Hebrews says, ' They without us are not made perfect.' His sense of loyalty to all who have preceded him in this karmic-cycle, urges him to do his part faithfully in carrying forward the torch and to pass it on, at least undimmed, to those rebirth appearances who will certainly follow after.

Nor does the Buddhist give up all hope of participation in future bliss. He recognizes that in him is the ' spark ' of the eternal Buddhanature that in the long last will be freed of its encumbering illusions of ignorance, and in the pure cognition of the Buddhahood participate in the identity of the Dharmakaya. He sees that the element of eternality is not in his particular ego-self, which is only appearance after all, but is rather in his karmic idea-form and spirit that ever change but endure until all desires of ignorance and illusion that have appeared in his body, are ' burnt out ' at Nirvana, when the ripple will find itself to be the ocean of the Buddha-nature. In fixing one's attention on this eternal ocean that is Buddahood, one thinks less of his transient appearance as body and self, and at death lays it down without regret.

Buddhism teaches that everything is an expression, a rhythm, of the Dharmakaya which is Love in its harmonious Totality. In the physical life, Love reveals itself as energy, enthusiasm; in the psychical life it appears as recognition, awareness, insight; in the spiritual life, where all distinctions of particularity, of time and space, of subject and object, are overpassed it is ecstasy, blissful peace and equanimity. It is Gautama's Golden Eightfold Path that leads one into this experience of Love's identification. The Sixth of the steps — Right Effort — is but the wise response on the Physical plane to Love's dynamic call to good-will and service. The Seventh step — Right Meditation — is but the holding oneself receptive, on the Psychic plane to Love's intuition and Vision. While the Eighth step — Right Concentration — is but the glad yielding, on the Spiritual plane, to Love's urge to supreme unification and participation in the ineffable unity of Love's harmonious Wholeness.

Love is the Ultimate Principle, for it alone is universal, all-inclusive, infinitely reconciling, harmonizing, unifying, fusing. Always it is seeking to overcome discrepancies, discords, selfishness, oppositions, ever seeking to give form and freedom and soul and meaning and purpose and beauty to what otherwise would be ugly and inert and meaningless. At one stage it appears as energy, at another as life, at another as thought, at another as aspiration, but always it is everywhere present. Love is the only Reality, everything else is appearance.

The French philosopher, Emanuel Berg, in his masterly analysis, entitled the Nature of Love, detects three fundamental elements, dynamism, awareness, and fusion. This trinity of elements is seen also by Whitehead, the keen philosopher of Nature, in his book, Religion in the Making. He asserts that religion is man's reaction to his solitariness. These reactions register on three faculties, experience, meditation, intuition; and from them he learns that there are three corresponding elements in all nature, namely, in the physical world of experience, the presence of a creative energy; in the psychic world of cognition, the presence of a tendency to form and meaning; and in the spiritual world of concentrated intuition he detects the presence of a principle of ' concretion ' by reason of which the universal enters into and determines each particular. Professor Wieman writing in the New Republic concerning Professor Whitehead's book, remarks,

If we define God as Love, the principle of concretion seems to state our meaning. For what is universal Love if it be not the ordering of all being in such a way that it can enter most fully into the existence of every particular thing. If God be the principle of concretion in the universe, then love is the fullest actualization in human life of the divine order, and the best adaptation that man can make to that which is God. If we define God as beauty, the principle of concretion still holds good. For is not beauty precisely this entrance of all parts into each part? Harmony, rhythm, beautiful form, are these not just different ways of indicating the principle of concretion.

Professor Whitehead insists that solitariness and meditation is a necessary element of religion, because thereby alone does one come to realize that rich concretion, that focusing of much reality, which only the loving heart can discern when pondering over what has been seen and thought and felt and heard in relation to the whole.

It means that one must isolate himself in order to digest what he has seen and heard and felt. In order to ponder these many things in the heart and gather up their larger significance and integrate more profoundly the meanings of the people with whom one associates and the culture of the day, one must be alone . . . . (and unless we are) the principle of concretion cannot freely operate in our midst, nor become manifest to our discernment. — (*Wieman.*)

The writer of John's Gospel shows the Divinity of Love; in the Letters of Paul there is a wonderful description of the resources and marvels of Love; and Plotinus has enneads upon Love that will always remain classic. But it is one of the values of Love that it comes to the humblest and most limited of mortals with its gifts of boundless energy and insight and ecstasy and compassion and fairly compels him to know more about Love from experience, and to give him more of experience of its tenderness and beauty, than John or Paul or Plotinus could describe.

It is Jesus' picture of God as the Heavenly Father, in whose loving care not one bird falls to the ground unnoticed, or one flower blossoms imperfectly, or one heart faints from weariness or neglect, without his knowledge and sympathy, that makes the idea of God lovely and lovable. John says that Jesus in foretelling the immanent presence of the Holy Spirit, called it The Comforter; and Paul and Peter spoke of the fellowship of believers whose lives 'were hid with Christ in God.' In the Last Supper as related by John, Jesus prayed: ' That they may all be one; even as Thou, Father, art in me, and I in Thee, that they also may be in Us.'

The corresponding conception in the mind of Gautama was the Dharmakaya, the all-inclusive ' Suchness' of blended Truth and Love. It is this Dharmakaya that is everywhere immanent. Its loveliness is seen in all things both great and small; in animal and vegetable life, mutually dependent and mutually serviceable; in humanity at its best, kindly, thoughtful, sympathetic and helpful, co-operating in good-will for the common good; in saints, enlightened and enlightening; in Bhodisattvas, boundless in wisdom and compassion; in Buddhas, full of grace and truth.

With the final step of the Golden Path there comes the spiritual insight and the radiation of loving kindness for the blessing of all animate life. Then follows sympathetic gladness and perfect equanimity, calm and peaceful even-mindedness. On the physical plane it is the dynamism of compassion and loving kindness; on the psychical plane it is the awareness of sympathetic gladness; and on the spiritual plane where all dividing lines of you and me, of mine and thine, where the thing loved and love itself are merged in one, and all distinctions are done away with and have disappeared, Love must reveal itself as perfectly disinterested equanimity.

Tirumular, a Saivite saint, writes:

> The ignorant say, Love and God are different;
> None know that Love Itself is God.
> When they know that Love Itself is God
> They will rest content in Love.

We believe that Jesus, unconsciously, had been influenced by Buddhism. We believe that it was from that source that Jesus derived, indirectly, his conception of God as Love, as the Heavenly Father rather than as Jehovah, Lord God Almighty; or, as the writer of John's Epistles definitely says: God IS Love.

CHAPTER SEVENTEEN

DID JESUS FOLLOW THE GOLDEN PATH?

THAT Jesus was one of the world's great Saviors, there is no dispute. Some even believe that he is THE world Savior. The latter, if they are followers of Pauline and Johanine Christianity, base their belief on the theistic doctrine and ecclesiastical dogma that Jesus was the Only-begotten Son of God; and that as such ' there is no other name given among men whereby we must be saved.' Or, as it is written in John's Gospel, ' For God so loved the world, that he gave his Only-begotten Son, that whosoever believeth on him should not perish, but have eternal life. . . . He that believeth on the Son hath eternal life, but he that believeth not on the Son shall not see life, but the wrath of God abideth on him.'

This is pure doctrine and dogma and is, of course, incapable of proof. It must be accepted by faith in the Bible or on the authority of the Church. Others base their belief on this doctrine and dogma on the evidence of miracles which Jesus did, and especially on the great miracles of the resurrection and ascension of Jesus; or on the miracle of transubstantiation in the Eucharist, by which the physical elements of the bread and wine are alleged to be changed into the actual body and blood of the risen Christ. Or, as Uhlmann defends in his book, on the absolute sinlessness of Jesus. Or, as many do, upon the immaculate conception of the Virgin Mary by the Holy Ghost. This line of belief is also wholly incapable of test and proof, resting as it does for any evidential value it may have upon the historical records of the New Testament which as we have already seen have very little evidential value, or upon the authority of ecclesiastical councils whose decisions are often very dubious and human.

Many Christians believe that Jesus was the Only-begotten Son of God on the evidence of their emotions before, at or after their conversion. But even this is now considered to be of doubtful evidential value, as the scientific study of the human mind is revealing its proneness to suggestion and wish-to-believe, and the mental habit of rationalizing its beliefs as against all assaults from without.

On the contrary, Buddhist scholars generally are perfectly willing to accept Jesus as being a genuine Bodhisattva, one who has obtained enlightenment and his right to Nirvana but who, because of his deep and loving compassion, is determined to forego that privilege until he can bring all animate life with him. Many of the wisest Buddhist scholars are perfectly willing to count Jesus as a Buddha, and accord him equal honor with all other Buddhas, on the ground that Jesus has evidently followed the Golden Path, disciplined his desires, obtained enlightenment, and victory over the thirst for selfness, has achieved spiritual insight, gracious compassion and finally found on the cross his Nirvana.

This generous belief of Buddhist scholars, as it is based on the more easily accessible facts of his life, can therefore be more safely examined and evaluated. It depends largely on the fact as to whether Jesus did, or did not, wittingly or unwittingly, follow the Golden Path. Let us examine the life of Jesus in this aspect.

The First Step of the Gold Path is, Right Ideas. What do the Buddhists consider Right Ideas? The Four Noble Truths, of course. The first is, ' All things which have a cause are impermanent and lead to suffering.' The prophecies of the Old Testament foretold that the coming Messiah would be a 'suffering Servant,' ' a man of sorrows and acquainted with grief.' The records everywhere note the fulfillment of this prophecy in Jesus' life; it was replete from childhood to death with apparent failure, physical suffering and the bitterness of lack of understanding and appreciation from those he loved and came to serve. His own introvert nature,

his immediate relatives, the crowds that first followed and then left him, the religious leaders and
authorities of his day who persecuted him and
sought his death, all tended to unhappiness and
suffering. Finally in Gethsemane there was the
agony of recognized failure, and on the cross the
overwhelming pain of physical suffering, and the
still more poignant mental agony of the sense of
desertion which led him to cry out, ' My God,
why hast thou forsaken me? '

The Second of the Noble Truths was this:
' That all suffering is caused by clinging to the
illusions and thirsts and desires of the senses, the
mental processes, and the spiritual illusion and
thirst for selfness.' Jesus certainly practised and
taught a decided restraint of the desires. The
Seven Beatitudes ascribe blessings on all those
who at heart are meek, hunger after righteousness more than comfort, are merciful, pure in
heart, peacemakers, and suffer for righteousness'
sake. That is, Jesus taught that the blessed life
is not in the material satisfactions of life, or the
abundance of things possessed, but rather consists in the voluntary resignation of them for the
good that follows. He calls those who make
this relinquishment and practice this restraint,
' the salt of the earth ' and ' the light of the
world.' He explicitly says that it is because of
this restraint that they are enabled to enter the

Kingdom of Heaven. His distinction between the act of lust and the desire cherished in the heart and mind, reveals the same basis of conviction. It is the one who is non-resistant to evil that is living the good life; it is the one who is cherishing no favorites or publicity in his benevolences; nor who clings to friends before enemies; nor who seeks honor and praise for his religious prayers, who is his follower. He distinguishes the treasures of the good things of earth from those laid up in heaven by a life of self denial, because thereby the heart is freed from its natural clinging. He solemnly warns them against any anxious desire for even the so-called necessaries of life, food and clothing, and even of physical life itself. He boldly asserts that if the carnal desires are beyond conscious control, one better sacrifice the eye or the right hand, than to be overborne by them. He utters the parable of the good tree bearing good fruit, to show how impossible it is, if the heart is filled by selfish desires, to resist bearing evil fruit. When the scribe offered to follow him, he warned him that to do so meant privation, and when the rich young man asked what he must do to be perfect, Jesus replied that he must dispose of his wealth and accept the burden of poverty and privation. He asks, ' What shall it profit a man if he gain the whole world and lose his own soul?' He asserts that the love of money is the root of all evil; that it is harder for a camel to go through the eye of a needle, than for a rich man to resist the desires of the body. In reply to a question about marriage, he asserted that for those that could bear it willingly, the celibacy of the homeless life was better. When he sent out the Twelve Disciples on a special mission, he insisted that they take no extra food, clothing or money, that they accept whatever hospitality was offered. When Peter reminded Jesus that for his sake they had left wives and children, and lands and homes, he commended them and assured them of the future reward of eternal life. He taught that the finding of the truer, higher life of spirit entailed the first relinquishing of the lower, experiential life. So conspicuous is the emphasis that Jesus places on the life of self denial that Nietzsche, the severest critic that Christianity ever had, based his judgment on what he called the slave morality of Jesus. To Nietzsche it was the polar opposite of the masculine will-to-power that he thought to be biologically desirable. Nevertheless it approved itself to Jesus' mind, and was essentially the same that Gautama taught in the Second and Third Noble Truths.

The Third Noble Truth was this: There is a way to end this clinging to the thirsts of the illusions of lust, ignorance and selfness. Much that has just been written about Jesus' attitude toward the Second Noble Truth involves his attitude toward the Third and need not be repeated. But in addition Jesus taught explicitly that while the way to the satisfaction of the physical life was broad and open, the way to the freer and higher life of spirit was narrow, and that few were those that found it. But he urged everyone to seek for it and assured them that every one who honestly sought his way would certainly find it.

The Fourth Noble Truth, Gautama asserted, was that the way to get rid of this clinging was to follow the Golden Eight-fold Path. There is absolutely no evidence that Jesus ever heard of this by name, but the way that Jesus himself followed and that he offered to others is so much the same in essence that one is forced to admit that from his Essene days he had learned about it and absorbed its substance. The Way of Jesus as distinguished from the Way of Gautama was the omission of these Four Noble Truths. Jesus practised them to be sure and taught others to do so, but failed to impress upon his followers that they were an essential part of his Way of Love. In the mind of Paul the essential thing of Jesus' way of life was its general *spirit* of love. The Path that Christianity has offered is the way of love as being sufficient in itself to safeguard life's destiny, leaving the widest liberty to individual beliefs as to basic truths. Jesus said that the great commandments were two, love to God and love to the neighbor. He said, ' By this shall all men know that ye are my disciples, if ye have love one for another.'

And in words of tenderest sympathy he urged men to follow his way. ' Take my yoke upon you and learn of me,' he said, ' for I am meek and lowly of heart; and ye shall find rest unto your souls. For my yoke is easy and my burden is light.'

Paul interpreted the way of Jesus to mean obedience to a spiritual law of righteousness, as opposed to the physical law of sin and death. The writer of John's Gospel saw it to mean a mystical faith in the person of the Risen Christ. He writes that in answer to Thomas's question, Jesus replied: ' I am the Way, the Truth, and the Life, no man cometh unto the Father but by Me.' But these are later interpretations of disciples who had become accustomed to the spiritualization and deification of the person of Jesus, seeing in the Risen Christ the Only-begotten Son of God. There is nothing in the actual words or manner or method of Jesus' life and teachings to give basis to them. He simply enunciated the Law of Love as a practical rule of life, and that

involved a denial of the lusts of the flesh and the
pride of life and selfness.

The Second Step is Right Aspiration, or
Right Resolution. Jesus most certainly took
this step at his baptism. It was the crucial moment in his life, the moment when all the dreams
and desires of his soul took form and resolution.
And this resolution remained unshaken to the
end. It endured the temptation in the wilderness, the misunderstandings and lack of appreciation on the part of the multitudes he tried to
serve. It endured the discouragement that came
with the failure of the Twelve to awaken general
recognition. It survived the conviction that came
to him that his own mission was futile and that
only with his death would the Kingdom come. It
endured the rejection at the temple, the agony
in the Garden when the near approach of a
shameful death taxed his utmost devotion. It
endured the final agony on the cross. Certainly
Jesus had taken the Second Step.

The Third Step is Right Speaking. While
there are some words spoken by Jesus when he
was tormented by the Pharisees that seem to be
spoken in anger and impulse, far more generally
his words were winning and gracious, full of
tender kindness and affection. It is recorded
that even those sent to arrest him gave evidence
' that no man ever spake as this man.' Another

record says, 'He spake not as the Scribes and
Pharisees, but as one having authority.' Even
the high priests were baffled at his silence, and
Pilate marvelled at his composure. At one time
he said to his disciples, ' Out of the abundance of
the heart the mouth speaketh; but, I say unto
you, that for every idle word that men shall
speak, they shall give account thereof in the day
of judgment; for by thy words thou shalt be
judged, and by thy words thou shalt be condemned.' And his cousin James, who was himself an Essene follower of John the Baptist, and
who later, after the death of Jesus, became leader
of the Jerusalem followers of Jesus, said, ' So
also the tongue is a little member and boasteth
great things. Behold how much wood is kindled
by how small a fire. And the tongue is a fire:
the world of iniquity among our members is the
tongue, which defileth the whole body and setteth
on fire the whole of nature and is set on fire by
hell.' In another place he says, ' Let every man
be swift to hear, slow to speak, slow to wrath.'
' If any man thinketh himself to be religious and
bridleth not his tongue, but deceiveth his heart,
this man's religion is vain.' Paul speaks of words
without love as ' clanging cymbals and sounding
brass,' and urges his followers always ' to speak
the truth with love.'

The Fourth Step is Right Action. As the

Buddhist ethical commandments are similar to the Jewish Ten Commandments and other ethical ideals we would naturally expect Jesus to be observing them. The Buddhist commandments are as follows: not to kill, not to steal, not to commit adultery, not to lie, not to drink intoxicating drinks, not to eat between meals, not to attend secular entertainments, not to use oils, perfumes or jewelry, not to use ' soft ' beds, not to handle money. Besides these there are hundreds of other precepts, as for instance, not to slander, not to insult, not to be avaricious, to all of which Jesus was obedient.

In addition Gautama taught the necessity for those who were intent to reach the highest advancement of self-discipline, to forsake the household life and private property and to live the strictly chaste and disciplined life of a monk, wandering about, healing the sick and by good conversation teaching the good law, and doing deeds of kindness to everyone without discrimination, depending upon and accepting hospitality as offered, and spending much time in solitary meditation. Jesus' early association with the Essenes led him to follow all these rules.

The Fifth Step was Right Livelihood. The Buddhists counted the homeless life of the monk the highest vocation, and this Jesus followed. He spoke of it once with great pathos, ' The

foxes have holes and the birds of the air have
nests where they may rear their young, but the
Son of Man has nowhere to lay his head.'

The Sixth Step was Right Effort. This involves the spirit of one's behavior. The Buddhists say that the result of right effort will be the
Ten Graces: *kindness* to all without discrimination, control over those acts and mental habits
that endanger *serenity* of mind, *patience* under
the irritating things of life, *zeal* in perfecting
the monk's calling, *tranquility* under either success or failure, comfort or adversity, *calm insight* as opposed to the temptation to mental distraction or argument or assertion, *sympathy* that
includes tactfulness and resourcefulness, *devotion* to the highest ideals of wisdom and compassion, *fortitude* or the courage to face and endure every evil influence or untruth of persecution, *wisdom* that comes from meditation rather
than from erudition, from intuition rather than
from intellect, a spiritual intuition that enables
him to comprehend and explain the ultimate nature of things from immediate awareness. We
will take space to enumerate only a few passages
to show that Jesus had achieved these graces,
limiting ourselves to the final grace of the wisdom that comes from spiritual insight. In
John's Gospel, where it records the visit of the
learned Nicodemus to Jesus by night, after

Nicodemus had hesitated at something that Jesus had asserted, it is written,

Verily, verily, I say unto thee, we speak that which we know, and bear witness of that which we have seen; and ye receive not our witness. If I told you earthly things and ye believe not, how shall ye believe if I tell you heavenly things?

And in another place it is written, according to Moffat's translation,

Jesus, however, would not trust himself to them: he knew all men and required no evidence from anyone about human nature; well did he know what was in human nature.

There are also the other quotations which we have already quoted referring to the authority with which he spoke.

The Seventh Step is Right Meditation. Jesus was noted for the frequency with which he went off by himself to meditate and pray and from this habit he gained immeasurably in the graces mentioned in connection with the Sixth Step.

The Eighth Step is Right Concentration. That Jesus took this step in his solitary vigils of prayer there can be little doubt; he certainly revealed the fruits of it in his supreme spiritual insight, in his gracious compassion, in his sympathetic gladness, and in his surprising equanimity and calm assurance under his final trials and crucifixion. The records give only one instance

of trance and ecstasy, that of his transfiguration
on the mountain, when it is recorded that his face
shone with the glory of it.

The illusion of selfness was the most difficult
of the clingings for Jesus to relinquish, and this
is not to be wondered at when we recall his introvert nature, his Jewish inheritance of a coming messiah, and the universally present psycho-
logical ideas of his day.   But at last that, too,
gave away, perhaps even more than his companions noted or the records recorded.   By the
anguish in the Garden of Gethsemane we see
how hard it was to give up his will to the Divine
Will, but he did it.   And on the cross, when his
poor tortured body cried out in agony, may we
not think that he yielded the last vestige of that
clinging, when he cried, ' Into thy hands I commit my spirit? '

The Golden Path starts with the admission of
the fact that all suffering comes from clinging
to the illusions of the mortal life, of which the
hardest to get rid of is the idea of self; it is a path
of restraint and release from the trammels of
lust, ignorance and selfness; its goal is a gradua
awakening, increasing of enlightenment and
deepening sense of identity with the Divine.

It is not suggested that Jesus had any definit.
knowledge of Gautama's Golden Path, or con
sciously followed it; what is suggested, is, tha

unwittingly he did follow it, and attained its goal of final unity with the Divine. And if one aspires to be a follower of Jesus, he, too, ought to be following it.

But the historic Christian Church have chosen to follow another path, namely, the path of intellectual belief in doctrines and dogmas of theistic legalism, which has a basis of egoism in its conception of an independent and eternal conscious soul. This leads all Christians to an exaggeration of egoism and a desperate clinging to its illusion of an eternal life. This path is a divided path, for on the one hand it is a path of ethical idealism and self restraint, but on the other hand it is a path of acquisition, of ' getting ' all the comforts and indulgencies of the senses and the mind and the selfness that its ethical code allows. The effort to follow both paths leads to the Christian's undoing. The conventional Christian thinks and prays and sings of a ' giving up ' that in his heart of heart he hopes will never be necessary. His path of ethical self restraint never relinquishes that final clinging to selfness. It is rather a path that fosters egoism by its ethical education and training, which ever holds out the hope of getting some magical learning, or virtue or grace that will enable him to locate and follow the narrow way, without actually giving up any creature comforts or favorite illusion;

with one hand putting fuel on the fire and when it blazes up trying to quench it with the other hand. Trying to follow this divided path inevitably results in self deception, unrest, sophistry, and casuistry. Professor Robinson asserts that three-quarters of all mental activity is given up to this bad habit of rationalization, trying to convince one's self that his favorite ideas are right. A man deludes himself with the idea that there is nothing wrong in his particular desires, and so he becomes dissatisfied with his position, or his wife does, and seeks a more remunerative position and calls it a ' larger field,' a ' place of greater usefulness.' He yields to questionable means or policy or finesse or deceit, and justifies it by the name of ' the greater good he can accomplish' with the added power or wealth. ' The end justifies the means ' becomes an insidious balm to his conscience. To be the minister of a great church, to be a cardinal-archbishop, to be a great scholar, a great benefactor, a great philanthropist, even to be 'the Messiah;, is an almost irresistible temptation, just so long — and no longer — as that last thirst for selfness is cherished.

The Way of Jesus is the way of Love. He nobly taught the universality of the Law of Love as a guide to the good life. And it *is* a safe

guide to those who first admit the Four Noble
Truths — the universality of suffering, its cause
in a clinging to the thirsts of mortal selfness. But
when one clings to that idea of an immortal soul
he follows Dante,

In the midst of this our mortal life I found me in a
gloomy wood, astray, gone from the path direct, and e'en
to know the way it were no easy task.

Even Jesus, himself, dallied with that temptation in its most insiduous form — to be the
Messiah — and he clung to it desperately, but
because he was honestly following the Golden
Path he was saved from being overborne by it.
Inch by inch the delusion of selfness yielded,
he 'sweat blood' toward the end, but yield at
last it did; and Jesus found, at last, the rest its
yielding always brings.

There is no more pathetic scene in all the Gospels than that given in John's Gospel of his
brave struggle to find release. In the account of
the final appearance of Jesus to his disciples in
Galilee, it is written that after his death the disciples had returned to their former callings and
three of them had been out fishing all night with
no results. As day broke they returned to the
shore and to their amazement saw Jesus standing patiently in the chill mists of the dawn. He
had built a little fire and had food cooking for

them. After they had eaten he talked with them humbly, childishly, almost incoherently, and the burden of his words was this, ' Peter, feed my lambs, feed my sheep.'

No, the Golden Path is a path of restraint and resistance to the thirsts of the impermanent body and conscious mind. There can be no other starting point. It leads to release from the human clinging to its illusions, and most particularly to its illusion of a suppositious eternal life for the conscious mind.

Even as Gautama said, this idea of an enduring conscious soul must be eradicated, rooted out, finished, ended, if one is ever to gain release from the sufferings of this life and break the endless chain of rebirths into the same conditions of mortality.

If one is prepared to give up this idea of an independent and eternally self-conscious soul, he may hopefully follow the Golden Path with entire loyalty to Jesus and his way of Love. To be sure, he must change certain of his former favorite ideas, as for instance, that Jesus was different from himself — that *he* came from above. He must give up Paul's frequent use of the simile of "fighting to win.' The spirit of Love is always a yielding, a giving up; it is never one of assertion and acquisition.

And that wonderful verse that the Second Century writer of John's Gospel puts into the mouth of Jesus, that, too, must be changed, if we are to get its full depth of meaning, if we are to follow the Golden Path in the spirit of Jesus, that must be changed to read,

Love is the way, the truth, and the life. No man cometh unto the Father, but by love.

Early Buddhism, by T.W. Rhys Davids. There is no better scholar to have outlined the early formation of Buddhism than T.W. Rhys Davids. The book is short, to the point, and filled with interesting facts. It is a step by step guidebook to what Buddhism really is and was intended to be, and is perfect for providing a complete overview of Buddhist origins. Paul Tice has contributed to this work with a short section entitled *Buddhist Ethics: The Way to Salvation?* In it he explains how Buddhism was not meant to be a form of religious worship, but an important system of ethics. When practiced properly, as the Buddha had done, this ethical system was meant to bring personal salvation. **ISBN 1-58509-076-X • 112 pages • 6 x 9 • trade paper • $12.95**

 *The Fountain-Head of Religion: A Comparative Study of the Principal Religions of the World and a Manifestation of their Common Origin from the Vedas,* by Ganga Prasad. This unique and interesting book puts forth the idea that all great religions of the world have come from a common source, and if that is the case then that common source would have to be the Vedas. The Vedas are the scriptures of the Hindu religion, thought by Hindus to have been written by wise men at the beginning of human history. The word "Veda" actually means "wisdom" or "knowledge." The goal of those who follow Vedic teachings is a union with God called *samadhi,* equal to nirvana for the Buddhists. The author traces the Vedas back to being the oldest written source of theology and, ultimately, the source of all other theological systems. He takes major religious themes like good and evil, the afterlife, resurrection, and the name used for God in Judaism, Christianity and Buddhism and traces them confidently back to the Vedas. This is an extremely important book that deserves to be studied closely by anyone interested in the origin of religions, their own beliefs, and the belief systems of others. **ISBN 1-58509-054-9 • 276 pages • 6 x 9 • trade paper • $22.95**

India: What Can It Teach Us, by Max Muller. Max Muller was one of the most respected religious authorities of his time. His accomplishments include translating The Upanishads and editing a massive collection of work called The Sacred Books of the East.. Some of the most valuable and instructive materials in the history of man are treasured up in India, and in India only. In her classic dialect, the Sanskrit, we may read with what success ancient India conquered the elements and the world as it was then known. The study of Sanskrit, and particularly a study of the Vedic Sanskrit, is able to enlighten us and illuminate the darkest passages in the history of the human mind. This book gives the reader some idea of ancient India, of its ancient literature, and, more particularly, of its ancient religion. Muller will help you see and feel what it was like in ancient India, and the importance that it played in the history of the human race. **ISBN 1-58509-064-6 • 284 pages • 5 1/2 x 8 1/2 • trade paper • $22.95**

 *Triumph of the Human Spirit: The Greatest Achievements of the Human Soul and How Its Power Can Change Your Life,* by Paul Tice. A triumph of the human spirit happens when we know we are right about something, put our heart into achieving its goal, and then succeed. There is no better feeling. People throughout history have triumphed while fighting for the highest ideal of all -- spiritual truth. Tice brings you back to relive and explore history's most incredible spiritual moments, bringing you into the lives of visionaries and great leaders who were in touch with their souls and followed their hearts. They explored God in their own way, exposed corruption and false teaching, or freed themselves and others from suppression. Tice covers great movements and people who may have physically failed, but spiritually triumphed. This book not only documents the history of spiritual giants, it shows how you can achieve your own spiritual triumph. In today's world we are free to explore the truth without fear of being tortured or executed. As a result, the rewards are great. Various exercises will strengthen the soul and reveal its hidden power. One can discover their true spiritual source with this work and will be able to tap into it. This is the perfect book for all those who believe in spiritual freedom and have a passion for the truth. **ISBN 1-885395-57-4 • 295 pages • 6 x 9 • trade paper • illustrated • $19.95**

Of Heaven and Earth: Essays Presented at the First Sitchin Studies Day, edited by Zecharia Sitchin. ISBN 1-885395-17-5 • 164 pages • 5 1/2 x 8 1/2 • trade paper • illustrated • $14.95

God Games: What Do You Do Forever?, by Neil Freer. ISBN 1-885395-39-6 • 312 pages • 6 x 9 • trade paper • $19.95

Space Travelers and the Genesis of the Human Form: Evidence of Intelligent Contact in the Solar System, by Joan d'Arc. ISBN 1-58509-127-8 • 208 pages • 6 x 9 • trade paper • illustrated • $18.95

Humanity's Extraterrestrial Origins: ET Influences on Humankind's Biological and Cultural Evolution, by Dr. Arthur David Horn with Lynette Mallory-Horn. ISBN 3-931652-31-9 • 373 pages • 6 x 9 • trade paper • $17.00

Past Shock: The Origin of Religion and Its Impact on the Human Soul, by Jack Barranger. ISBN 1-885395-08-6 • 126 pages • 6 x 9 • trade paper • illustrated • $12.95

Flying Serpents and Dragons: The Story of Mankind's Reptilian Past, by R.A. Boulay. ISBN 1-885395-38-8 • 276 pages • 6 x 9 • trade paper • illustrated • $19.95

Triumph of the Human Spirit: The Greatest Achievements of the Human Soul and How Its Power Can Change Your Life, by Paul Tice. ISBN 1-885395-57-4 • 295 pages • 6 x 9 • trade paper • illustrated • $19.95

Mysteries Explored: The Search for Human Origins, UFOs, and Religious Beginnings, by Jack Barranger and Paul Tice. ISBN 1-58509-101-4 • 104 pages • 6 x 9 • trade paper • $12.95

Mushrooms and Mankind: The Impact of Mushrooms on Human Consciousness and Religion, by James Arthur. ISBN 1-58509-151-0 • 180 pages • 6 x 9 • trade paper • $16.95

Vril or Vital Magnetism, with an Introduction by Paul Tice. ISBN 1-58509-030-1 • 124 pages • 5 1/2 x 8 1/2 • trade paper • $12.95

The Odic Force: Letters on Od and Magnetism, by Karl von Reichenbach. ISBN 1-58509-001-8 • 192 pages • 6 x 9 • trade paper • $15.95

The New Revelation: The Coming of a New Spiritual Paradigm, by Arthur Conan Doyle. ISBN 1-58509-220-7 • 124 pages • 6 x 9 • trade paper • $12.95

The Astral World: Its Scenes, Dwellers, and Phenomena, by Swami Panchadasi. ISBN 1-58509-071-9 • 104 pages • 6 x 9 • trade paper • $11.95

Reason and Belief: The Impact of Scientific Discovery on Religious and Spiritual Faith, by Sir Oliver Lodge. ISBN 1-58509-226-6 • 180 pages • 6 x 9 • trade paper • $17.95

William Blake: A Biography, by Basil De Selincourt. ISBN 1-58509-225-8 • 384 pages • 6 x 9 • trade paper • $28.95

The Divine Pymander: And Other Writings of Hermes Trismegistus, translated by John D. Chambers. ISBN 1-58509-046-8 • 196 pages • 6 x 9 • trade paper • $16.95

Theosophy and The Secret Doctrine, by Harriet L. Henderson. Includes **H.P. Blavatsky: An Outline of Her Life,** by Herbert Whyte, ISBN 1-58509-075-1 • 132 pages • 6 x 9 • trade paper • $13.95

The Light of Egypt, Volume One: The Science of the Soul and the Stars, by Thomas H. Burgoyne. ISBN 1-58509-051-4 • 320 pages • 6 x 9 • trade paper • illustrated • $24.95

The Light of Egypt, Volume Two: The Science of the Soul and the Stars, by Thomas H. Burgoyne. ISBN 1-58509-052-2 • 224 pages • 6 x 9 • trade paper • illustrated • $17.95

The Jumping Frog and 18 Other Stories: 19 Unforgettable Mark Twain Stories, by Mark Twain. ISBN 1-58509-200-2 • 128 pages • 6 x 9 • trade paper • $12.95

The Devil's Dictionary: A Guidebook for Cynics, by Ambrose Bierce. ISBN 1-58509-016-6 • 144 pages • 6 x 9 • trade paper • $12.95

The Smoky God: Or The Voyage to the Inner World, by Willis George Emerson. ISBN 1-58509-067-0 • 184 pages • 6 x 9 • trade paper • illustrated • $15.95

A Short History of the World, by H.G. Wells. ISBN 1-58509-211-8 • 320 pages • 6 x 9 • trade paper • $24.95

The Voyages and Discoveries of the Companions of Columbus, by Washington Irving. ISBN 1-58509-500-1 • 352 pages • 6 x 9 • hard cover • $39.95

History of Baalbek, by Michel Alouf. ISBN 1-58509-063-8 • 196 pages • 5 x 8 • trade paper • illustrated • $15.95

Ancient Egyptian Masonry: The Building Craft, by Sommers Clarke and R. Engelback. ISBN 1-58509-059-X • 350 pages • 6 x 9 • trade paper • illustrated • $26.95

That Old Time Religion: The Story of Religious Foundations, by Jordan Maxwell and Paul Tice. ISBN 1-58509-100-6 • 220 pages • 6 x 9 • trade paper • $19.95

Jumpin' Jehovah: Exposing the Atrocities of the Old Testament God, by Paul Tice. ISBN 1-58509-102-2 • 104 pages • 6 x 9 • trade paper • $12.95

The Book of Enoch: A Work of Visionary Revelation and Prophecy, Revealing Divine Secrets and Fantastic Information about Creation, Salvation, Heaven and Hell, translated by R. H. Charles. ISBN 1-58509-019-0 • 152 pages • 5 1/2 x 8 1/2 • trade paper • $13.95

The Book of Enoch: Translated from the Editor's Ethiopic Text and Edited with an Enlarged Introduction, Notes and Indexes, Together with a Reprint of the Greek Fragments, edited by R. H. Charles. ISBN 1-58509-080-8 • 448 pages • 6 x 9 • trade paper • $34.95

The Book of the Secrets of Enoch, translated from the Slavonic by W. R. Morfill. Edited, with Introduction and Notes by R. H. Charles. ISBN 1-58509-020-4 • 148 pages • 5 1/2 x 8 1/2 • trade paper • $13.95

Enuma Elish: The Seven Tablets of Creation, Volume One, by L. W. King. ISBN 1-58509-041-7 • 236 pages • 6 x 9 • trade paper • illustrated • $18.95

Enuma Elish: The Seven Tablets of Creation, Volume Two, by L. W. King. ISBN 1-58509-042-5 • 260 pages • 6 x 9 • trade paper • illustrated • $19.95

Enuma Elish, Volumes One and Two: The Seven Tablets of Creation, by L. W. King. Two volumes from above bound as one. ISBN 1-58509-043-3 • 496 pages • 6 x 9 • trade paper • illustrated • $38.90

The Archko Volume: Documents that Claim Proof to the Life, Death, and Resurrection of Christ, by Drs. McIntosh and Twyman. ISBN 1-58509-082-4 • 248 pages • 6 x 9 • trade paper • $20.95

The Lost Language of Symbolism: An Inquiry into the Origin of Certain Letters, Words, Names, Fairy-Tales, Folklore, and Mythologies, by Harold Bayley. ISBN 1-58509-070-0 • 384 pages • 6 x 9 • trade paper • $27.95

The Book of Jasher: A Suppressed Book that was Removed from the Bible, Referred to in Joshua and Second Samuel, translated by Albinus Alcuin (800 AD). ISBN 1-58509-081-6 • 304 pages • 6 x 9 • trade paper • $24.95

The Bible's Most Embarrassing Moments, with an Introduction by Paul Tice. ISBN 1-58509-025-5 • 172 pages • 5 x 8 • trade paper • $14.95

History of the Cross: The Pagan Origin and Idolatrous Adoption and Worship of the Image, by Henry Dana Ward. ISBN 1-58509-056-5 • 104 pages • 6 x 9 • trade paper • illustrated • $11.95

Was Jesus Influenced by Buddhism? A Comparative Study of the Lives and Thoughts of Gautama and Jesus, by Dwight Goddard. ISBN 1-58509-027-1 • 252 pages • 6 x 9 • trade paper • $19.95

History of the Christian Religion to the Year Two Hundred, by Charles B. Waite. ISBN 1-885395-15-9 • 556 pages. • 6 x 9 • hard cover • $25.00

Symbols, Sex, and the Stars, by Ernest Busenbark. ISBN 1-885395-19-1 • 396 pages • 5 1/2 x 8 1/2 • trade paper • $22.95

History of the First Council of Nice: A World's Christian Convention, A.D. 325, by Dean Dudley. ISBN 1-58509-023-9 • 132 pages • 5 1/2 x 8 1/2 • trade paper • $12.95

The World's Sixteen Crucified Saviors, by Kersey Graves. ISBN 1-58509-018-2 • 436 pages • 5 1/2 x 8 1/2 • trade paper • $29.95

Babylonian Influence on the Bible and Popular Beliefs: A Comparative Study of Genesis I.2 by A. Smythe Palmer. ISBN 1-58509-000-X • 124 pages • 6 x 9 • trade paper • $12.95

Biography of Satan: Exposing the Origins of the Devil, by Kersey Graves. ISBN 1-885395-11-6 • 168 pages • 5 1/2 x 8 1/2 • trade paper • $13.95

The Malleus Maleficarum: The Notorious Handbook Once Used to Condemn and Punish "Witches", by Heinrich Kramer and James Sprenger. ISBN 1-58509-098-0 • 332 pages • 6 x 9 • trade paper • $25.95

Crux Ansata: An Indictment of the Roman Catholic Church, by H. G. Wells. ISBN 1-58509-210-X • 160 pages • 6 x 9 • trade paper • $14.95

Emanuel Swedenborg: The Spiritual Columbus, by U.S.E. (William Spear). ISBN 1-58509-094-4 • 208 pages • 6 x 9 • trade paper • $17.95

Dragons and Dragon Lore, by Ernest Ingersoll. ISBN 1-58509-021-2 • 228 pages • 6 x 9 • trade paper • illustrated • $17.95

The Vision of God, by Nicholas of Cusa. ISBN 1-58509-004-2 • 160 pages • 5 x 8 • trade paper • $13.95

The Historical Jesus and the Mythical Christ: Separating Fact From Fiction, by Gerald Massey. ISBN 1-58509-073-5 • 244 pages • 6 x 9 • trade paper • $18.95

Gog and Magog: The Giants in Guildhall; Their Real and Legendary History, with Account of Other Giants at Home and Abroad, by F.W. Fairholt. ISBN 1-58509-084-0 • 1 pages • 6 x 9 • trade paper • $16.95

The Origin and Evolution of Religion, by Albert Churchward. ISBN 1-58509-078-6 • 504 pages • 6 x 9 • trade paper • $39.95

The Origin of Biblical Traditions, by Albert T. Clay. ISBN 1-58509-065-4 • 220 pages • 5 1/2 x 8 1/2 • trade paper • $17.95

Aryan Sun Myths, by Sarah Elizabeth Titcomb, Introduction by Charles Morris. ISBN 1-58509-069-7 • 192 pages • 6 x 9 • trade paper • $15.95

The Social Record of Christianity, by Joseph McCabe. Includes *The Lies and Fallacies of the Encyclopedia Britannica,* ISBN 1-58509-215-0 • 204 pages • 6 x 9 • trade paper • $17.95

The History of the Christian Religion and Church During the First Three Centuries, by Augustus Neander. ISBN 1-58509-077-8 • 112 pages • 6 x 9 • trade paper • $12.95

Ancient Symbol Worship: Influence of the Phallic Idea in the Religions of Antiquity, Hodder M. Westropp and C. Staniland Wake. ISBN 1-58509-048-4 • 120 pages • 6 x 9 • trade paper • illustrated • $12.95

The Gnosis: Or Ancient Wisdom in the Christian Scriptures, by William Kingsland. ISBN 1-58509-047-6 • 232 pages • 6 x 9 • trade paper • $18.95

The Evolution of the Idea of God: An Inquiry into the Origin of Religions, by Grant Allen. ISBN 1-58509-074-3 • 160 pages • 6 x 9 • trade paper • $14.95

Sun Lore of All Ages: A Survey of Solar Mythology, Folklore, Customs, Worship, Festivals, and Superstition, by William Tyler Olcott. ISBN 1-58509-044-1 • 316 pages • 6 x 9 • trade paper • $24.95

Nature Worship: An Account of Phallic Faiths and Practices Ancient and Modern, by the Author of Phallicism with an Introduction by Tedd St. Rain. ISBN 1-58509-049-2 • 112 pages • 6 x 9 • trade paper • illustrated • $12.95

Life and Religion, by Max Muller. ISBN 1-885395-10-8 • 237 pages • 5 1/2 x 8 1/2 • trade paper • $14.95

Jesus: God, Man, or Myth? An Examination of the Evidence, by Herbert Cutner. ISBN 1-58509-072-7 • 304 pages • 6 x 9 • trade paper • $23.95

Pagan and Christian Creeds: Their Origin and Meaning, by Edward Carpenter. ISBN 1-58509-024-7 • 316 pages • 5 1/2 x 8 1/2 • trade paper • $24.95

The Christ Myth: A Study, by Elizabeth Evans. ISBN 1-58509-037-9 • 136 pages • 6 x 9 • trade paper • $13.95

Popery: Foe of the Church and the Republic, by Joseph F. Van Dyke. ISBN 1-58509-058-1 • 336 pages • 6 x 9 • trade paper • illustrated • $25.95

Career of Religious Ideas, by Hudson Tuttle. ISBN 1-58509-066-2 • 172 pages • 5 x 8 • trade paper • $15.95

Buddhist Suttas: Major Scriptural Writings from Early Buddhism, by T.W. Rhys Davids. ISBN 1-58509-079-4 • 376 pages • 6 x 9 • trade paper • $27.95

Early Buddhism, by T. W. Rhys Davids. Includes *Buddhist Ethics: The Way to Salvation?,* by Paul Tice. ISBN 1-58509-076-X • 112 pages • 6 x 9 • trade paper • $12.95

The Fountain-Head of Religion: A Comparative Study of the Principal Religions of the World and a Manifestation of their Common Origin from the Vedas, by Ganga Prasad. ISBN 1-58509-054-9 • 276 pages • 6 x 9 • trade paper • $22.95

India: What Can It Teach Us?, by Max Muller. ISBN 1-58509-064-6 • 284 pages • 5 1/2 x 8 1/2 • trade paper • $22.95

Matrix of Power: How the World has Been Controlled by Powerful People Without Your Knowledge, by Jordan Maxwell. ISBN 1-58509-120-0 • 104 pages • 6 x 9 • trade paper • $12.95

Cyberculture Counterconspiracy: A Steamshovel Web Reader, Volume One, edited by Kenn Thomas. ISBN 1-58509-125-1 • 180 pages • 6 x 9 • trade paper • illustrated • $16.95

Cyberculture Counterconspiracy: A Steamshovel Web Reader, Volume Two, edited by Kenn Thomas. ISBN 1-58509-126-X • 132 pages • 6 x 9 • trade paper • illustrated • $13.95

Oklahoma City Bombing: The Suppressed Truth, by Jon Rappoport. ISBN 1-885395-22-1 • 112 pages • 5 1/2 x 8 1/2 • trade paper • $12.95

The Protocols of the Learned Elders of Zion, by Victor Marsden. ISBN 1-58509-015-8 • 312 pages • 6 x 9 • trade paper • $24.95

Secret Societies and Subversive Movements, by Nesta H. Webster. ISBN 1-58509-092-1 • 432 pages • 6 x 9 • trade paper • $29.95

The Secret Doctrine of the Rosicrucians, by Magus Incognito. ISBN 1-58509-091-3 • 256 pages • 6 x 9 • trade paper • $20.95

The Origin and Evolution of Freemasonry: Connected with the Origin and Evolution of the Human Race, by Albert Churchward. ISBN 1-58509-029-8 • 240 pages • 6 x 9 • trade paper • $18.95

The Lost Key: An Explanation and Application of Masonic Symbols, by Prentiss Tucker. ISBN 1-58509-050-6 • 192 pages • 6 x 9 • trade paper • illustrated • $15.95

The Character, Claims, and Practical Workings of Freemasonry, by Rev. C.G. Finney. ISBN 1-58509-094-8 • 288 pages • 6 x 9 • trade paper • $22.95

The Secret World Government or "The Hidden Hand": The Unrevealed in History, by Maj.-Gen., Count Cherep-Spiridovich. ISBN 1-58509-093-X • 270 pages • 6 x 9 • trade paper • $21.95

The Magus, Book One: A Complete System of Occult Philosophy, by Francis Barrett. ISBN 1-58509-031-X • 200 pages • 6 x 9 • trade paper • illustrated • $16.95

The Magus, Book Two: A Complete System of Occult Philosophy, by Francis Barrett. ISBN 1-58509-032-8 • 220 pages • 6 x 9 • trade paper • illustrated • $17.95

The Magus, Book One and Two: A Complete System of Occult Philosophy, by Francis Barrett. ISBN 1-58509-033-6 • 420 pages • 6 x 9 • trade paper • illustrated • $34.90

The Key of Solomon The King, by S. Liddell MacGregor Mathers. ISBN 1-58509-022-0 • 152 pages • 6 x 9 • trade paper • illustrated • $12.95

Magic and Mystery in Tibet, by Alexandra David-Neel. ISBN 1-58509-097-2 • 352 pages • 6 x 9 • trade paper • $26.95

The Comte de St. Germain, by I. Cooper Oakley. ISBN 1-58509-068-9 • 280 pages • 6 x 9 • trade paper • illustrated • $22.95

Alchemy Rediscovered and Restored, by A. Cockren. ISBN 1-58509-028-X • 156 pages • 5 1/2 x 8 1/2 • trade paper • $13.95

The 6th and 7th Books of Moses, with an Introduction by Paul Tice. ISBN 1-58509-045-X • 188 pages • 6 x 9 • trade paper • illustrated • $16.95

9 781585 090273